T0322265

THE
CREATIVE
ENTREPRENEUR

By Carolyn Dailey

Contents

About the author

Carolyn Dailey is a leading figure in the creative industries. A communicator and connector, she is the founder of Creative Entrepreneurs (CE), a first-of-its-kind online community empowering creatives to grow brilliantly successful businesses. CE provides learning resources and inspiration for entrepreneurial creatives, translated into a language they can understand.

Fully immersed in the creative world, Carolyn connects creatives within the supportive community she is building that helps them pursue their full business potential. She has lectured and presented at foundational pillars of the creative world such as Central Saint Martins, The V&A, Serpentine Galleries, Whitechapel Gallery, Design Museum, London College of Fashion, London Design Festival, Cambridge University, Ravensbourne University and other leading institutions.

She has represented creatives across design, music, architecture, film, fashion, publishing, gaming and the other creative sectors to the heart of government at No. 10 Downing Street, including chairing its first ever Roundtables on Creative Entrepreneurship.

Carolyn has been named by *Creative Review* as one of the Top 50 Creative Leaders, by *WIRED* magazine as one of the Top 10 Women Digital Powerbrokers and by *BIMA* as one of the Top 10 Entrepreneurs progressing the creative industries. She regularly appears on SKY News commenting on the creative sector and brands.

Her expertise arose from her 20 years at entertainment leader Time Warner, whose portfolio included HBO, CNN, Turner, Warner Bros., Time Inc. magazines (*Time*, *InStyle* etc) and Warner Music. She was the company's top executive in Europe and worked to establish Time Warner's brand as the leading company of ideas.

Dedication:
To Ted Turner,
The Crazy One

Ted Turner is the ultimate creative entrepreneur and I had the privilege of working at his start-up. I saw him build what would become a visionary template for the future. First, he pioneered massive tech disruption, then he dreamt up creative disruption – creative business models that have given rise to the successes of Netflix and others today. But he saw it back in the 70s.

From when television was invented in 1926, there were very few channels operating over government controlled frequencies. When cable TV came along in the 70s, it was intended only to boost reception of these channels in obscure rural areas of America. Around the same time, Ted discovered that it had become possible to put programming on a satellite and beam it down across the country.

His brilliance was to connect these two new, seemingly unrelated tech innovations, and use them for purposes they weren't intended for; to broadcast local cable TV programming via satellite across America. With this vision, he created TBS, the first new national free TV channel since TV was invented.

Next came that creative content disruption. As a busy entrepreneur Ted didn't have time to watch the broadcast network news, served up only a few times per day. He wanted to be able to check the news any time. So he invented CNN.

I arrived at CNN in London in 1990 to work on yet another visionary idea of Ted's. As he was already producing CNN for America, why not put it on a satellite to make it available to Europe? Now it's a globally recognised brand.

It sounds blindingly obvious now, but when he launched CNN in 1980, it was both incomprehensible and revolutionary. He was mocked, the broadcast networks called it "Chicken Noodle News." It transformed not only the media, but the wider world. Just one example: its contribution to the fall of the Berlin Wall in 1989 and the tectonic socio-economic-political shifts that followed.

Steve Jobs didn't put Ted in his famous *The Crazy Ones* campaign for nothing. Alongside Albert Einstein, Martha Graham, John Lennon, Martin Luther King, Mahatma Ghandi, Muhammad Ali, Maria Callas, Frank Lloyd Wright and others, the campaign paid tribute to the people who, in Jobs' opinion, had changed the world and pushed the human race forward.

> ## The people who are crazy enough to think they can change the world… are the ones who do.

Steve Jobs

Ted wasn't going to stop there. He applied his 24/7 viewing logic to entertainment content. He often said: "I want to watch *Casablanca* any time I want, why do I have to wait until one of the traditional broadcast networks shows it, if they ever do?" Therein lay his next revolutionary vision.

No one saw the enduring value of great creative content after its initial release and distribution – after which the Hollywood studios typically deep-sixed their content, storing the physical celluloid "prints" in salt mines in Kansas (to preserve them), with their titles entered into databases which they called "libraries" – where they languished in the ether.

Ted was the one who saw that these libraries were the golden goose.

So he bought MGM's film library (*Casablanca, The Wizard of Oz, 2001: A Space Odyssey, Singin' in the Rain*) and Hanna Barbera's animation library (*Tom and Jerry, Looney Tunes, The Jetsons*). This was much to the consternation of his board of directors and financial analysts who all said he was massively over-paying for old content. In fact, these acquisitions turned out to be the deals of a lifetime.

From these libraries, he created 24/7 entertainment channels: Turner Classic Movies and Cartoon Network. In this act of creative genius, he took the creativity of many to a global stage, bringing much-loved content to people around the world. Ted created versions of these same entertainment channels for a European audience and launched them in the mid '90s – but not without a big diplomatic blow up in France. But why stop at what he had already created?

His next step was to produce new original content for his channels and to get into the feature film business himself by buying independent film studios. He bought Castle Rock Entertainment (*The Shawshank Redemption, Spinal Tap, Seinfeld*) and New Line Cinema (*The Golden Compass, Lord of the Rings, Elf, Dumb and Dumber*), which, combined with his Turner Pictures studio, created the first new "Hollywood Major" studio since the original five "Hollywood Majors" had taken shape in the 1940s.

The world changes at lightning speed, and exponentially now with the rise of Generative AI. But core values never change. Ted likes to say "Content is King". His core value has always been to bring brilliant creativity to his audiences, the same way that every creative entrepreneur in this book does.

I am eternally grateful to have had what I now see was a front row seat on history, watching a genius at work, along with his signature irreverence, rebellion, determination and mischievous humour. I learned the lessons of a lifetime. For that reason I dedicate this book to Ted Turner.

C ,

The people who are crazy enough
to think they can change the world…
are the ones who do.

Steve Jobs

C

INTRODUCTION

Who this book is for

Whether you have a creative business, are dreaming of starting one or are just curious about what this world of creative entrepreneurship looks like, this book is for you. It will give you a deeper understanding of what is possible for you and how to chart your own path.

And for those of you working at a company, you can be highly creative and entrepreneurial in a corporate environment, taking responsibility yourself for your own creativity and innovation. You can use your day job as a patron of sorts for your art – it lets you hone your creativity on the side without having to make a living from it, while also learning transferable skills. All of which can serve you if you do decide to take the plunge and build your own creative business.

In this uncertain world, no matter what position you are in, one thing is certain – injecting more creativity into your life is a sure winner.

Meet the people and ideas you need to know now

This book lets you hear directly from some of the world's most inspiring and innovative creative entrepreneurs about how they built their businesses. These are the untold business stories intended to let you see yourself represented, to inspire you and to give you actionable business advice from these people who have done it.

This book is also a call to adventure, to invite you to think about creativity from a new perspective – not purely about the creative discipline itself, but about how creativity can form the basis of a successful business, or a new way of looking at your career, which can let you take your creativity, and your life, to new heights.

Within each interview I have added "**Takeaways**" to reinforce key points our creative entrepreneurs make, and to make it easier for you to come back to the book later and skim through it quickly to review highlights.

Between the interviews, I have added what I call "**Business Essentials**." These are checklists summarising the key business topics that every creative entrepreneur needs to know about. It's of course not possible in the space we have to cover all business topics, or to cover them in depth, but these are the top priorities which give you a snapshot of what you need to know.

I hope that from this book you take away a huge amount of inspiration from hearing the original and personal stories directly from these remarkable creative entrepreneurs.

I hope you will be amused, amazed and enlightened. And, on a personal note, I hope you enjoy, as much as I have, spending time with them and getting to know them. I hope you feel like you're sitting at the dinner table with us. So, pull up a chair.

How this book came about

Like so many things in life which turn into passions for their creators – penicillin, Post-It notes, Play-Doh (which comes up later in this book), chocolate chip cookies and Velcro – this book happened by accident. Or, as Nile Rodgers would say, Hippie Happenstance. I can't claim any hippie cred, but you get the drift.

I spent my whole career in the creative world, starting in TV working under Ted Turner at his revolutionary CNN in London, which was soon joined by his new entertainment channels and movie studios. Through various machinations and mergers, I moved to Turner's parent company Time Warner, which also oversaw HBO, Warner Bros., Time Inc magazines and Warner Music.

While having the privilege of seeing the output from these creative hotbeds and working with the most amazing people across them, I also got to work on some of the biggest milestone challenges for the creative sector as it evolved from being a tightly controlled country-by-country affair, to living in the global, borderless, freely accessible world of the internet. Which meant working with incredible creatives and others across the industry spectrum, and in many cases forming lifelong connections.

Through all of these experiences, I took away two key principles. First, that business could be the enabler of creative vision, rather than the other way around. And second, that if you bring together a committed and collaborative community, you can solve nearly any problem. These two principles would become the foundations of Creative Entrepreneurs.

To bring these two principles to life, I can tell you the stories of a few of these milestone challenges, one at the beginning and one at the end of my experiences which led me to start CE.

The first one was in the mid-90s. Europe had embraced the idea that all TV content should move freely across national borders. So we launched Turner Classic Movies and Cartoon Network across Europe. As we celebrated, the French said "*non*", shutting down the channels in France when they saw the reality, seeking to protect their French content. This was against the law. We reeled. What just happened? We'd followed all the rules. Ted threatened to stop drinking French wine.

We could choose to fight for years in court or find another path to get our business back up and running in France. Eventually, in his abiding wisdom, Ted said "You know what our mistake was? This was not a business problem or a legal problem or a creative problem – this was a diplomatic problem, and we didn't have anyone in charge of diplomacy. Carolyn is going to be in charge of that now."

Working with brilliant Turner colleagues, we jumped into action and brought together a formidable alliance across the UK film and television industries. This was, after all, a threat to all non-French creators and had the British creative world freaked out as well. Connectivity and diplomacy were to win the day. The culmination was a visit by Ted to London with his then wife, Jane Fonda. We met with Tony Blair, the newly elected Prime Minister who was championing the creative industries. It was an epic meeting. The Turner channels were restored in France. The might of a collective creative alliance was established.

Fast forward to 2010. Along came the new internet giants Google and Facebook offering virtually all content online for free. This included professional content – not just cats on skateboards, but the likes of *Harry Potter* and other content that cost hundreds of millions to produce and upon which hundreds of thousands of people depended for their livelihoods. These new online players were eating our lunch in the court of public opinion, portraying themselves as the Robin Hoods robbing from paid content services and "selflessly" giving it away to the masses.

This drew the creative sector together and partnerships were once more the answer. Everyone's IP was under threat, whatever the creative discipline. It was my job to lead the Time Warner diplomatic charge from London. Working together with my great Time Warner colleagues and across the creative sectors, we succeeded in getting legislation passed in the UK recognising that professional content online has to be valued and paid for. As the UK is one of the world's most respected creative economies, this changed the game, establishing this principle around the world.

As life returned to normal at a big corporation, I left to start my own creative agency, enthused to continue working across all the creative sectors. I knew exactly what I wanted to do creatively: put brands together with creativity to tell their stories. But very soon I learned I didn't know what I didn't know about the start-up side of a business. Yes, from Ted I knew how to spend no money, be scrappy and protect IP, but I'd never been exposed to the other entrepreneurial sides of his business, like raising money and financial forecasting.

I obviously must be missing something, I thought, as so many creative businesses had grown into huge global brands. I started asking around to my friends across the sectors, many of whom had built those brands. To my surprise, every single person – not some, not many, but *EVERY* person – said that, in the beginning, they hadn't known what they were doing on the business side, or who to ask or where to find information in a language they could understand. They all said that, looking back, they saw they'd made unnecessary stupid mistakes and hadn't grown as fast as they could have. I also clocked in every conversation, everyone's eyes would light up, so triggering was the concept of needing business support in the beginning, which they hadn't had.

At the same time, I knew a lot of people in tech and they were regularly going to events where they could be connected with mentors, potential investors and peers pursuing the same dream. I thought, why isn't there the same support in the creative sector? It's the second biggest contributor to the UK economy (after financial services) and is massively commercially successful – by some measures more successful than the US creative economy.

Around this time, I was invited to a meeting at the Arts Council. Unlike in the US, there is substantial government-backed funding for the creative sector in the UK, and the Arts Council is one of the biggest sources of it. The meeting was to press the Arts Council to encourage its community of arts organisations to think more about building sustainable creative businesses rather than living hand to mouth from grant to grant.

At the meeting, I suggested there should be at least a baby step of a website where creatives could come to find basic business resources, in a language they could understand. To my surprise, the head of the Arts Council said, "Great idea, we want to give you a grant to build that website." I had only meant I thought it was a good idea; not that I should do it! But now I had to get it done, and after much casting around with web developers, I did.

I called this fledgling site "Creative Entrepreneurs" and we launched it at No. 10 Downing Street in 2016. The launch generated a great deal of awareness – which was the goal – including articles in *The New York Times, Architectural Digest, Evening Standard* and others, which spread the word widely.

The response was unexpectedly overwhelming. We received messages from people around the world asking when we could bring Creative Entrepreneurs to their country. As demand continued to grow, we expanded the Creative Entrepreneurs offering, including an event series where I interviewed high-profile creative entrepreneurs about how they built their businesses, held in creative spaces where creatives could feel at home. After a few years, it became my full-time enterprise.

The two core principles mentioned above – using business to enable creativity and building a collaborative community – became the foundations of our mission.

A few years later, I was minding my own business when – by happenstance – we received an email in the public mailbox of Creative Entrepreneurs. Dorling Kindersley said they loved what we were doing and would like to discuss a book based on its mission. It was a daunting thought – I'd never written a book. But I saw it as a once-in-a-lifetime opportunity to tell the stories of the most inspiring creative entrepreneurs, to provide much-needed role models, and to pass on their concrete advice and wisdom.

So that's a long way of explaining how this book came about. As a first-time writer who thrives on collaboration, sitting in a room by myself writing it has not been easy. But with the challenges, I have learned so much and my biggest wish is that, from reading it, you do, too.

The Creative Entrepreneur Manifesto

We need to give business support for creative people a radical makeover and show that building a successful business empowers creativity. We want to build a supportive community and a vibrant economic environment where creative entrepreneurs from any background can achieve their full potential.

This is a call to arms for the creative community everywhere.

Here are the key principles that our community and the wider world can rally around to bring this goal to life – it is our Manifesto and we hope you join us in putting it into action.

We want to...

1. <u>Raise awareness</u> of the commercial potential of creativity.

- Demonstrate the huge and growing commercial success of the creative sector.

- Show creatives, parents and educators the commercial potential of creative entrepreneurship.

- Show investors that creative businesses that are scalable offer excellent investment opportunities.

2. <u>Celebrate role models</u> who show what is possible.

- Tell creative entrepreneur stories that demonstrate success in creative businesses.

- Provide a platform for these role models to share what they've learned.

- Start wider conversations about creative business.

3. Shift the <u>mindset</u> around creativity.

- Challenge stereotypes of creatives as hobbyists and starving artists.

- Show that making a living from creativity is empowering and possible.

- Fight the idea that creativity and commerce are at odds – good business lets creative vision take flight.

4. Build a joined up <u>supportive ecosystem</u>.

- Build a vibrant and nurturing community for up-and-coming creative entrepreneurs.

- Connect creative business experts, mentors, peers, investors and more.

- Create a space where those who have made it in the creative industries can give back.

5. <u>Provide business support</u> creative people can relate to.

- Speak in a business language that creative people can understand.

- Empower creatives with learning and networking resources they can easily access.

- Connect creative business experts with people who are starting out.

6. <u>Increase accessibility</u> for people of all backgrounds.

- Show a new path into the creative industries via starting a creative business.

- Empower people facing traditional barriers to gain access for themselves through entrepreneurship.

- Tell the stories of creative entrepreneurs from all backgrounds.

C

LAY OF
THE LAND

← Thomas Heatherwick's
"Little Island" - a
public park and outdoor
performance space just
off Manhattan's West Side
Highway in the Hudson River

First, what do we mean by "creative"?

Descartes famously said: "I think, therefore I am". In reply, I'd say: "I am human, therefore I am creative". Creativity is an essential characteristic which exists within each of us. The Oxford English Dictionary defines creativity as "the use of imagination or original ideas to create something; inventiveness."

It's what we humans do. From a pilot finding a way to land safely after an engine fails to a farmer finding new ways to grow crops in the face of climate change; from a banker working out how to compete with the crypto world to a commuter navigating an ingenious way around the traffic, or a parent inventing a game to stop their baby from crying. We're all built for creativity and practise it every day.

↓ Chair from Yinka Ilori's collaboration with fashion brand MCM

↘ Claire Foy and Matt Smith star as Queen Elizabeth II and the Duke of Edinburgh in *The Crown*, produced by Andy Harries

Aside from using "creative" to describe this innate human quality, there's also a more specialised use of the word in an economic or cultural context, where it is used to describe a particular category of activity that produces output based on the imagination. We talk about the "creative sector", the "creative industries", or the "creative economy". While the meanings of these terms have some technical differences, they refer to roughly the same thing. In this book, for simplicity, we'll mainly use "creative sector", which includes music, film, TV, video games, art, architecture, fashion, design, publishing, performing arts and marketing/advertising: industries that all involve creative people and the creative process.

↓ White Fender
Stratocaster guitar, as
used by Nile Rodgers

↘ Roksanda SS23 Runway
at the Serpentine Pavilion
"Black Chapel" designed
by Theaster Gates, London
Fashion Week October 2022

The creative sector's output is based on human creativity, which generates intellectual property (IP). For example, a film comprises a myriad of individual creative outputs: writing, cinematography, set and costume design, make-up art, etc. All are brought together in one "product", which is then "consumed" by an audience. So while all humans are creative, in this book, when talking about "creative entrepreneurs" we are talking about people who have started businesses in the creative sector.

How creative entrepreneurs are different

Creative entrepreneurs tend not to fit the mould of your typical entrepreneur. Most don't even think of themselves as entrepreneurs in the first place. Ask them what they do, and they'll tell you: "I'm a fashion designer", "I'm a film producer", "I'm an architect", "I'm a musician". In fact, in the creative sector, the word "entrepreneur" tends to carry negative connotations, conjuring up images of tech-bros or cigar-smoking, mega-yacht-owning masters of the universe.

Mainstream entrepreneur:

"What's your exit strategy?"

Creative entrepreneur:

"My life's work is to build something beautiful for people to enjoy."

For a creative person, their driving motivation is to get their creativity into the world. Most focus first and foremost on their creative discipline – the business side tends to be secondary – only later do they realise they can make a livelihood from it. And they normally aim to steer away from "the business side" as much as possible, often just muddling through it. Which can also mean leaving themselves vulnerable to exploitation and failing to reach their full potential.

Moreover, their values are different: they're about creative integrity and connecting emotionally with audiences. In other words, they flip on its head the standard thought process of the mainstream entrepreneurial world.

In that world, the starting point tends to be the other way around: first a desire to make a lot of money and then a search for an idea to achieve that. I learned that when I started my own business, naturally meeting people also building theirs. The contrast became even more apparent to me.

 I'm sure that I could be much more commercially successful had I taken different decisions, but money is not the motivator for me.

Amanda Levete, founder, A_LA Associates Architects

What an eye-opening experience for someone from the creative sector, struck by the swagger of mainstream entrepreneurship – this was a whole new world.

I first observed that mainstream entrepreneurs tend to love business, both the idea and the practice of it, that's their main focus. I learned that they particularly relish being "Founders", defining themselves as such with an almost messianic zeal. In fact some even believe that the lowest position on the food chain is being an "em-ploy-ee" (each individual syllable pronounced with emphasis).

"What's your exit strategy?", "Have you done your Series A?" "What's your burn rate?", "Do you have your MVP?", "What's your post money valuation?", "How steep is your hockey stick?", "Do you have product-market fit?", "What's your inflection point?"

This is the language and these are the questions I found bandied about with a fair amount of macho strut pulsing under the surface.

 Toto, I have a feeling we're not in Kansas anymore.

Dorothy to her dog Toto in *The Wizard of Oz*

I thought, *wow, people in the creative sector really do not think this way*. To them, creativity comes first, business is typically a "necessary evil".

Creative entrepreneurs sell products of the human imagination, which break down largely into either storytelling (film, TV, video games, music, publishing, performing arts, marketing & advertising) or design (fashion, architecture, design, craft), although of course these categories expand and overlap. These are all products that appeal to human emotion: the movie that makes you cry, the dress that makes you feel empowered, the book that changes your world view. While there may be algorithms involved in some areas (think TV streaming), for the most part these are products shaped by instinct, taste and emotional connection.

This means that creative entrepreneurs tend to be interested in the exceptional. While their products can often be scaled for a mass market with huge commercial success, their guiding purpose is to produce something unique. And unlike the "move fast and break things" motto of tech start-ups, they don't tend to release their products until they consider them perfect.

All of this can affect their commercial success. Their business cycles and potential scalability tend to be more unpredictable than in other sectors, meaning it can be harder to secure investment, although many don't even want it.

Creative entrepreneurs often struggle commercially, given that they don't tend to have business backgrounds, networks, mindsets, or, most crucially, role models, exactly what this book provides. Creatives need to see themselves modelled in the world as running successful enterprises, using business to enable their creative vision to reach its full potential.

We want to redefine the word "Entrepreneur" – and for that matter, the word "Founder" – in a way that creatives can relate to and embrace – thereby breaking down a fundamental misunderstanding, that business and creativity don't – and shouldn't – mix.

WHAT CREATIVE ENTREPRENEURS ARE NOT

~~MASTERS OF THE UNIVERSE~~

~~TYCOONS~~

~~MOGULS~~

~~WHEELER DEALERS~~

~~SPECULATORS~~

~~BIG SHOTS~~

~~IMPRESARIOS~~

~~SHOW OFFS~~

~~FAT CATS~~

~~TOP DOGS~~

The huge opportunity

Good business empowers creativity. But poll a room and ask which of the following has business potential: a new app to add funny facial expressions to your photos or a feature film. Most would likely choose the former.

On a daily basis, we're intimately engaged with what creativity produces, whether it's that playlist that energises us on our commute or the fashion that turns our heads in the street. Arguably, the products of creativity are the ones we are most emotionally connected to. They give us joy, entertainment, inspiration, expression and open our minds to new worlds. But how do all these creative treasures come to be? Is there money involved somewhere along the way? Is it distasteful to even ask, somehow spoiling the illusion that these fruits of artistic genius are sprouted from a creative mind and magicked into our lives?

Money is involved, and big time. This is important for anyone to know, but most crucial for those who are interested in a creative career yet fearful that they can't make a living from it. The creative sector is a powerhouse of commercial success globally, generating 3 per cent of the world's GDP. And at an accelerating rate, growing faster than most parts of the economy worldwide.

 According to UN estimates, the creative industries generate annual revenues of over $2 trillion and account for nearly 50 million jobs worldwide.

The Policy Circle

And the future of creative careers is looking even brighter, with technology offering a mass of new opportunities we're only just starting to grasp.

Not only is the creative sector a major driver of the world economy, but it also creates fulfilling jobs, enhances our overall wellbeing and is a standard-bearer for innovation. It is also the industry of the future; creativity is a sustainable, renewable resource coming from the human imagination.

Listening to mainstream conversation, however, you'd never know about the sector's outsized economic value. A key reason is that "business" remains a dirty word in the creative sector – at best a boring distraction from creativity; at worst a creative sell-out.

Quite the opposite is true. It is by harnessing business that people enable themselves to bring their full creative vision to life. Business is the servant, not the master, of bringing creativity into the world. That this isn't more widely understood is damaging in a number of ways.

Many people don't realise that they can build a career out of their creativity, instead assuming they must restrict it to a hobby. Parents commonly discourage their children from entering the creative sector, fearing they'll be destined to become "starving artists". Educators are under pressure to cut creative subjects from the curriculum because they are not perceived as commercially valuable to young people. Policymakers fail to grasp the economic power of the creative industries, often lumping them together with the publicly supported arts (think state-funded museums and art galleries) rather than the business sector where they belong.

It is a misunderstanding on an epic scale. For creative people, this means a mass of untapped potential and unrealised dreams. For the world at large, this means greatly diminished access to the delight and inspiration derived from the full range of creativity that could (and should) be out there.

The creative sector is massively commercially successful. And by embracing business, people can not only make a living, but they can make their creative dreams come true.

If you didn't know already, hopefully you're inspired to discover what a commercial success story the creative sector is.

The Creative Entrepreneur – telling the untold story

To recognise yourself in someone else's story – to see your similarities and to learn that they've achieved goals you want to achieve – can be life-changing. When people see a role model they can relate to, someone who shares their world view and values, they start to see themselves in them and imagine that they can do it too. For a creative person, seeing someone who has built a successful creative business is an empowering lesson. It lets them begin to see how business empowers their creativity, how they can overcome the business obstacles and how they shouldn't be ashamed to talk about the business side of their creative endeavour.

These role models for successful creative businesses are sorely lacking. While there are endless role models for creativity, on the one hand, and for entrepreneurship, on the other hand, there are virtually none for "creative entrepreneurship". If someone has a creative business – a fashion label, an architecture practice, a video game company – we tend to hear all about their creative output, but virtually nothing about how they built the business that makes it possible.

 That's what inspires me is hearing people's stories.

Yinka Ilori

This is the reason I started Creative Entrepreneurs. We started an event series, conversations with inspiring creative entrepreneurs. Everyone was desperate to learn from their entrepreneurial journeys. The response was "queue-round the block" huge. I met as well with investors, educators, media, cultural leaders and professional advisors. It became evident that the most urgent

→ One of the Roundtables on
  Creative Entrepreneurship,
  the first to be held at
  No. 10 Downing Street

↓ Carolyn Dailey
  interviewing architect
  Amanda Levete about her
  entrepreneurial journey in
  front of an audience of
  aspiring creatives in the
  main lecture hall of the
  V&A museum in London

#CreativeEntrs

issue in creative entrepreneurship was the gaping hole in awareness about the commercial success of, and opportunities in, the creative sector. The most effective way to fix that is to showcase creative entrepreneur role models who have been largely hidden so far. The most compelling and accessible way to learn about creative businesses – and anything, really – is through the stories that inspiring people tell.

 I couldn't see anyone doing what I was doing, starting a business from their creativity.

Priya Ahluwalia

Creative people are the ultimate storytellers – spinning tales in our favourite languages of music, fashion, film, design and art. These are the stories that move us, touching all our senses and emotions. The business backstories of creative entrepreneurs are gripping – precisely because they are the stories of such unlikely entrepreneurs, in the typical sense of the word. They rarely set out on that entrepreneurial path, but instead, being led by creative passion, have found their way, by hook or by crook, to entrepreneurial success.

The creative entrepreneurs I've chosen for this book embody all of this and more. As the curator of voices to take us on our journey, I wanted to focus on people who have created something wholly unique, in each case giving us a new way of seeing the world. Equally they demonstrate a world class enterprising acumen, despite their starting point being creativity. It's that magic combination of creativity with a business foundation that enables it.

Beyond that, the choice was a combination of instinct, serendipity and admiration for extraordinary creative talent – all of these factors forming the lens through which to determine who would tell the most inspiring, enlightening, engaging and educational stories.

Equally important to me was the juxtaposition of the creative entrepreneurs brought together in this book. I saw this as a way to create a fascinating and educational theoretical conversation among them, as a way to let their ideas bounce off each other to give deeper insight. So, I've chosen entrepreneurs from across the creative sectors and across generations. How interesting, I thought, to hear how Nile Rodgers' views compare with Roksanda Illincic's, or Andy Harries's with Priya Ahluwalia's.

While the contrasts are fascinating, I often saw that they were only "parlance" deep. Even with very different endeavours, these entrepreneurs articulate surprisingly universal themes: the importance of staying true to yourself; the need for collaboration; a talent for storytelling; an instinct for sensing the zeitgeist; willingness to take feedback; and a creative starting point that finds its way to business gradually, perhaps accidentally.

Each of the entrepreneurs included has a fascinating story that will help and inspire anyone reading this book. They are open and passionate about what they do, and also about passing on their knowledge to help those following in their footsteps as well as anyone interested in an insider's tour of what building a creative business is about.

So it's with great enthusiasm that I bring you the stories in this book, and with great gratitude that the interviewees let this book be the vehicle. I hope you are fascinated, entertained, inspired and educated.

NILE RODGERS

The Hitmaker

3

Nile Rodgers

Founder of The Chic Organization

If you've been on a dance floor over the last 40 years, odds are it was Nile Rodgers' music that got you out there. Jazz, disco, new wave, R&B, soul, electronic, hip-hop, rap and nu-soul – you name the genre, he has pioneered its sounds and made its defining hits. He first broke into the charts in 1977 with his own band Chic, who soon after produced the now-iconic "We Are Family" for Sister Sledge.

He went on to produce and collaborate with artists from a mix of genres and eras, from Diana Ross, David Bowie, Madonna and the B-52s, to Duran Duran, Daft Punk, Lady Gaga, Beyoncé and Coldplay. With his signature sound seducing audiences over decades, he has sold over 500 million albums and 75 million singles and generated over $2 billion of hit music – all originating from "The Hitmaker", his iconic Fender Stratocaster guitar.

While high-powered glamour and colossal success might be his vocation, they weren't his beginnings. He was born in New York City to a teenage mother, and it was through sheer talent and fortitude that Nile found his own way to turn his creativity into a living. And then a major business enterprise, The Chic Organization, which in its earliest days, after massive success, survived a cultural backlash against disco so extreme it threatened to kill his career.

A cultural icon, he is also a thinker, global influencer and activist fighting for climate education, racial equality and a better deal for artists in the age of streaming. His ability to constantly reinvent himself alongside the artists he collaborates with is the true source of his own inimitable brand of Creative Entrepreneurship.

I spoke to Nile at Le Crib, his recording studio in Westport, Connecticut.

↗ Coachella 2024, Nile Rodgers performing with K-Pop sensation LE SSERAFIM, wearing custom looks designed by Louis Vuitton's Artistic Director, Nicolas Ghesguière

↓ Nile Rodgers: Highlights

- First record deal with Atlantic Records for Chic's "Dance, Dance, Dance" in 1977
- 6 Grammy Awards, including Grammy Lifetime Achievement Award in 2023
- Inducted into the Rock and Roll Hall of Fame and the Songwriters Hall of Fame
- Chairman of the Songwriters Hall of Fame
- Chief Creative Advisor, Abbey Road Studios in London
- Has composed music for theatre, films such as *Coming to America* and video games such as *Halo*

- Co-Founder of the We Are Family Foundation which recognises, funds and mentors youth leaders who work to bring about positive change
- Has a mini planet – "Nilerodgers (191911)" – named after him by the International Astronomical Union (IAU)

Early days

I was raised in New York City. My parents were the sweetest people, they were hip intellectual beatniks. I came to music naturally because my biological father was an extremely accomplished musician, a percussionist, and my mother and her husband – the father who raised me – were both seriously into jazz. Music was something that was always around me; it was part of the culture and part of my environment.

My formal musical training was part of the standardised American school curriculum at the time, which only taught classical music – so if it wasn't a symphonic instrument it wasn't taught. Because my parents were heroin addicts, I never stayed in the same school very long. I was given whatever instrument was lacking in each new school orchestra I ended up in. By the time I was 14, I could orchestrate [arrange and score music] because I knew how every instrument in a symphony orchestra functioned.

The b-flat clarinet was my favourite. This turned out to be fantastic when the hippie movement rolled around in the 1960s and guitars became the thing, because the b-flat clarinet has the same written range as the guitar, so I could immediately transfer all of my musical training to the guitar. That gave me a leg-up on many guitar players my age.

↓ Nile Rodgers with characters from *Sesame Street*, in whose house band he got his first professional music job

'

Music was something that was always around me; it was part of the culture and part of my environment.

Nile Rodgers

"Yo, my man, lose my number"

When I was 19 years old I got my first big break as a professional musician playing guitar with the touring band for *Sesame Street*, and then also playing with the house band for The Apollo Theater in Harlem. Around that time a friend passed on the number of a bass player she knew. "He's got a good vibe," she told me, "I know you want to put together a band, you two should have a call." But when we spoke, he didn't take well to my super hippie, avant-garde ideas, and said "Yo, my man, lose my number" – that's a direct quote – and hung up on me.

A few months later, I was playing in a pick-up gig (in which no one knows each other) and I thought the bass player, called Bernard, was incredible. It turns out he thought I, the guitar player, was incredible. At the end we traded numbers and I said, "I never want to do a gig without you." After that, we were inseparable. One day, as we were on the subway going to a rehearsal we bumped into the friend who had passed on the number to me. She said, "I see you cats finally hooked up!" And Bernard said to me, "That was you on the phone?!"

Nothing changed my life like meeting Bernard Edwards. I now had a partner that believed in me and we believed in each other. We were such different people, and had our ups and downs, but we adored each other. We were partners until he died in 1996.

TAKEAWAY   **This underlines the key importance of meeting as many people as you can to increase the odds of finding your core network of collaborators and supporters, who will be not only crucial to your business success, but also to your happiness, sense of community and professional satisfaction.**

Chic is the word

Bernard and I formed The Big Apple Band and slogged away to get it off the ground, mainly playing backup for other bands. While playing gigs in London, my girlfriend suggested we go and see her favourite band, Roxy Music. I'd never heard of them, but when they came out on stage, I thought, *Whoa, what is this?* Not only was their music really cool, but they were wearing couture clothes, which was really unusual – they looked like models in a fashion ad – and the whole performance was super stylish and avant-garde. I was mesmerised. I called Bernard and said, "We've got to do the Black version of Roxy Music!" Seeing them perform made me realise that the art direction of our band would be almost as important as the music. We created Chic with this inspiration, as a totally immersive artistic experience, from the fashion to the sound.

Hearing me describe this experience, Bernard came up with the idea that the band should be called "Chic" – which I thought sounded funny, but I went with it. We set out to make a hit record. We had to plan for success, even though almost everything fails, but we treated it as if it was going to work. And it did.

Getting things in motion: "Everybody Dance"

As Bernard thought of the band's name, I wrote its first song – "Everybody Dance" – and we made a demo recording. All the biggest downtown DJs loved it, so it became a big hit in the downtown New York clubs.

The next thing was to do an official recording, which we definitely did not have the money to do. We had a friend called Robert Drake who was a DJ and also a maintenance man at a state-of-the-art recording studio and, fortunately for us, a fan of Chic. One night we roped in some friends, including R&B icon Luther Vandross, and Robert snuck us into the studio, paying the elevator operator $10 not to tell anyone. We recorded "Everybody Dance" all in one night.

TAKEAWAY **When you see something you have created start to break through, it's key to capitalise on that. Think about how you can turn it into a bigger success for your business, for example, in this case, creating a high quality professional version of it that you can then show to wider audiences.**

A few weeks later, Robert – who had made the recording that night – called me from the club where he was DJing and said, "You've got to get down here, you won't believe this, I can't explain it." When I arrived, Robert played "Everybody Dance" and the crowd let out a blood-curdling scream and filled the dancefloor – and stayed for continuous replays for longer than an hour. I was mesmerised, I was like "Wow, this is my song and these people are going crazy."

So, of course we tried to get a record deal for "Everybody Dance". We brought record executives down to this club so they could see the crazy reaction to it, the same thing would happen every night. But it didn't get us a record deal.

↖ Nile Rodgers and David Bowie
at the Frankie Crocker
Awards at the Savoy in New
York in 1983, the year
"Let's Dance" was released

↑ Nile Rodgers and his Chic
co-founder, bassist Bernard
Edwards, at legendary New
York recording studio Power
Station in 1983

← The band Chic – Bernard
Edwards, Norma Jean Wright,
Nile Rodgers and Tony
Thompson – pictured in 1977

The breakthrough milestone: "Dance, Dance, Dance"

Unable to get cash any other way, we borrowed $3,500 from some heavy tough guys to cut "Dance, Dance, Dance". It was a singles deal, meaning it had to be a hit or there would be no Chic.

Someone had told us the formula for getting a hit record was basically a mathematical one, which made me light up. The key was to be on one of the top radio stations in the No. 1 media city, New York. And then, like throwing a rock into a pond, the waves would break into concentric circles, as people would start talking about it there and it would get picked up by more radio stations across more cities and then, hopefully, the world. That made sense to us; it was logical.

We knew we couldn't break the top radio stations in New York. It was the most competitive market in America, and being Black, we only had one lane to drive down – if you weren't on the No. 1 Black station, you were irrelevant. So, being totally unknown, we said, let's go to Pittsburgh; a big city, but not a big *media* city.

TAKEAWAY

When a seemingly unmovable roadblock appears, that's when things get interesting. How can you work around it, not accepting the conventional rules, but finding a new way around it? For example, seeing new opportunities or reframing how to see the issue.

As a teenager I was working at Van Nuys airport in LA, used mostly by private jets. I would sometimes see Frank Sinatra there. He once told me, "Hey kid, why do you think it's called show business? You've gotta put on a show to do the business." So, we went to Pittsburgh and we put on a show.

The "Yowsah, Yowsah, Yowsah" interjection in the song is a reference to Depression-era American dance marathons. So for our meeting with the radio station programme director, we hired a girl in a 1920s flapper costume and a guy with a megaphone shouting: "Yowsah, Yowsah, Yowsah," while she danced around. We had little plastic megaphones, onto which we'd slapped the Chic logo, that we left behind as swag.

The programme director liked it and put the song on the station – and the phones just lit up with people requesting it. Because of the huge popularity in Pittsburgh, we ended up being played in New York exclusively on a brand-new radio station. The song was so hot that the station was rivalling the No. 1 New York station in terms of listener numbers, and was being talked about as the song turning America upside down. Atlantic Records jumped on the sensation and signed us to a record deal. In Mr. Sinatra's words, we did the business. As they say, the rest is history.

The Chic Organization

Playing backup for other bands, Bernard and I learned the fundamentals of how to build a successful music production business – not that we understood it as that at the time. After we got our record deal, we put together a corporation that would manage the band and all of its future enterprises: The Chic Organization Ltd.

Now that we were real, with a record deal, we had to demonstrate that the two young ramrods at the helm of the company could make this a viable new business. Bernard and I were co-owners of The Chic Organization and we paid everyone who played with us as salaried employees – not the normal structure for a band. The reason was that no one believed in us, so they preferred cash upfront to ownership in our company. This proved to be a good thing in the long run, as it let us keep our structure lean and simple.

The Disco Sucks implosion

And then suddenly, in the summer of 1979 – at the same time "Good Times" and our biggest hit ever "Le Freak" were topping the charts – the Disco Sucks movement erupted. Astonishingly, it was started by just one DJ from a local radio station in Chicago who had been fired when the station changed from rock to disco. Bitter about his own misfortune, he generated a backlash against disco that spread like wildfire, culminating with Disco Demolition Night, when this DJ called fans onto the field of a Chicago baseball stadium to burn disco records. We felt the brunt of it, cast as the enemies of rock and roll (when in reality we felt we were a subset of it), and it was harsh. The backlash was so toxic that people in the industry, even people benefitting massively from dance music, were afraid to be associated with us. What we didn't know when the Disco Sucks movement hit, and we were in the depths of despair, was that the owners of The Chic Organization Ltd. would go on to make even more hits than we had in the early years – the best was yet to come.

↑ Nile Rodgers with Daft Punk at the 56th GRAMMY Awards in Los Angeles, 2014, where they performed GRAMMY-winning "Get Lucky" with Pharrell Williams and Stevie Wonder

→ Lady Gaga and Nile Rodgers paying tribute to the late David Bowie during the 58th GRAMMY Awards, 2016

It's inevitable that totally unexpected challenges will hit your business at some point, some more extreme than others. While obviously no one welcomes these, it's crucial to retain unshakable confidence in your core talents and your ability to find your way through it. Depending on the circumstances, this can take a lot of time without the certainty of a clear path forward. It's so important to keep the faith that you will eventually figure it out by continuing to seek out opportunities based on your unique skills.

I'm coming out

Every record I did up until Disco Sucks was a success. And thank God we'd already signed our contract with Motown to work with Diana Ross. We were so associated with disco that, had we not had that contract, Barry Gordy (the Head of Motown) would never have let us produce what wound up being Diana Ross's biggest album of her life – *Diana*, featuring "I'm Coming Out" and "Upside Down".

Diana's success brought me and Bernard back into the business, even though Chic continued to be stigmatised and never had another hit.

"Nile, darling..."

David Bowie and I met by chance at the Continental, an after-hours club in New York, and bonded over jazz. What most people don't know is that he'd been dropped by his record label. It's hard to imagine that such a phenomenal artist actually had declining sales. At the end of the day, the record labels care about money and his sales weren't robust enough to keep him on.

When he started talking to me about working together, I got all excited thinking he wanted to do an experimental jazz album. But he said to me: "Nile, darling, I want you to do what you do best – I want you to make me a hit album." I thought, *That's so not a Bowie record to me*. But then I thought, with Bowie, a "pop hit" with people dancing to it, that's an art project. So I said, "Yes, this is awesome, I'll do it."

He invited me to his house in Lausanne, Switzerland, to work on it. When he played me an initial version of what he thought the hit "Let's Dance" could be, it sounded like a weird folk song – not a hit at all. So I said, "David, do you mind if I do an arrangement?" And he said, "Yes, great!" I completely rewrote the song and, through my friend who started the Montreux Jazz Festival, arranged to use Queen's recording studio right down the road, plus three back-up musicians.

In the studio, I handed David the sheet music for what I had composed and said, "Can you sing this version of your song while we play?" He did, and he absolutely loved it. We did the first cut of the whole album in two days, including "Modern Love" and "Cat People". He never really had a hit record up until I did *Let's Dance*. It was the top-selling album of his career.

"We want to make a record as if the internet never existed"

I'd originally met Guy-Manuel and Thomas of Daft Punk at a listening party in New York in the late '90s where they told me they were dedicating their album to Bernard, who had recently passed away. We talked about getting together again soon after that, but it didn't work out, so I just thought, *Oh well, it wasn't meant to be.*

↓ Nile Rodgers at London's historic Abbey Road Studio, where he is their first and only Chief Creative Advisor

Fast forward 15 or 20 years later and Daft Punk were in New York again. They came to my apartment and told me about the concept of *Random Access Memories*, which they wanted to work with me on.

> We have to learn how to live with failure because failure's going to be the great teacher.

Nile Rodgers

They said they wanted to make an album as if the internet never existed. I knew immediately what they meant and it blew me away: all live instruments with the best session musicians. And it meant long songs like "Let's Dance" or Chic's "Good Times", where we would make these main singles the longest songs on the album.

Being involved with that project was so monumental to my life. I won my first Grammy for it. And after that, I started playing with much younger artists like Charli XCX, Burna Boy and K-Pop sensations LE SSERAFIM, BTS's j-hope and the current biggest rock band in the world, Coldplay. Life was one way before *Random Access Memories* and completely different after.

Playing collaborations live keeps audiences contemporary

I play all The Chic Organization songs we collaborate on live, from "We Are Family", which we wrote for Sister Sledge, to Diana Ross, David Bowie, Madonna and Beyoncé. I have a rule – I never play an artist's song that I've worked on until after they've played it first. And then I Chic-ify it for our performances. This keeps my audience contemporary, as the audiences for all these collaborations love to hear us perform the songs live.

There's "influential", then there's "massively influential", then there's Nile Rodgers... a true innovator who never slows down, still making history with his guitar.

Rolling Stone

You know you've made it when...

When I played at the Prince's Trust for the first time, Prince Charles (before he was King Charles) said to me, "Nile, I don't know any of your music, but everybody seems to like it." And I said, "No, honestly, you do know it." Years later, as part of the Coronation celebrations in 2023, the Palace put out his top Spotify playlist. And the number three song was one of mine: Diana Ross's "Upside Down". So, when I was with him recently, I said, "Remember when you told me you didn't know my music – you just don't read the credits!" I didn't rub it in – well, I did rub it in. I said: "and 'We Are Family' and 'Let's Dance' – that's why everyone is dancing at your party!"

↓ Passing on lessons learned

People may say, "What can I learn from Nile Rodgers, he's a natural creative genius, everything he touches turns to gold (more like platinum) – what does that have to do with me?"

So not true. The majority of my work is failure. I have way more failures than I have successes, and I think that's normal. More businesses fail than succeed, so I'm no different than anyone else. The fact that I do a lot of business, you can pre-suppose that there will be a lot of failures. Every now and then, it's successful. It's crucial to realise this so that when failure comes, it's not a shock – instead, you understand it's part of the process of experimenting with what works and what doesn't, which you'll never know until you try. And if it turns out to be a failure, not letting it get you down into the depths and hinder your progress, but instead taking away what you can learn from it. The important thing is to keep going and have faith that you'll find what's right for you and your skills.

APPROACH EVERYTHING AS A HUGE SUCCESS... BUT ALWAYS HAVE A PLAN B

Every project I go into, I know the odds are against me. But I always approach it as if it's going to be the most successful thing I've ever created. If you believe in it and prepare for it that way, that's the best way to ensure you get your best results. Understand, though, that as most things don't work out, you have to have a Plan B, a Plan C, as a backup. Then, while aiming for the top, if it doesn't work out, you don't get too down about it, as you understood that was the likely outcome. That's what kept me and Bernard going; we never got too down.

FAILURE, THE GREAT TEACHER

I'd always say to Bernard: "We have to learn how to live with failure because failure's going to be the great teacher. We won't learn anything from success. If we're successful right away, we're going to think we know what we're doing – and we don't!" We only had instinct, we have to learn from failure.

YOU WANT TO MAKE YOUR SALAD TASTE GREAT

You want to do it for the art, but you need to have an audience. You have to have good instincts and have your fundamentals down, but you can't be dogmatic about it. Be open to feedback. You can say, "I believe in this, but it probably would be better if we added a little spice to it. It's cool, it's intellectual, it's primal – but is it catchy?"

You have to always think, *how do I make this extra interesting or eye-catching?* That's how you become relevant in your space, and when that happens it's amazing. It's what makes people want to buy your products, watch your films, hire you to design something. What I always wait for, after doing this now for about 50 years, is that moment when I play someone a song they haven't heard before and they want to hear it again. You want to make your salad taste great.

LOW OVERHEADS, HIGH PRODUCTIVITY

It's absolutely crucial to keep your overheads as low as possible. It lets you maximise what you can do with the revenues you make – having to spend as little of them on overheads as possible – and also survive the down times when not much revenue is coming in. Taking the example of The Chic Organization, the supply chain in the music business was dependent on so many people, places, and things lining up just right, but we rewrote the rules. We got rid of as many outside variables as possible. We started out downsized. Our overhead was low, and the return on investment was very high. Our early investors and business colleagues all did very well.

I made David Bowie's *Let's Dance* album in 17 days total, start to finish, and Madonna's *Like a Virgin* album in three weeks. On that score, it turned out to be lucky that I didn't have any experience other than what I call "making Black records". Our budgets were so low compared to a rock band's. They could rent a studio "locked out" meaning they'd have it for several days with all their stuff laid out for whenever they wanted to use it. Whereas Black records, we'd go in and make them in an eight-hour shift in one day.

The budget for my first album was $3,500 and I had the New York Philharmonic players and all these famous people on the album – because it was people whom I went to school with and people who were now famous. And they would teach me how to do a record for like no money.

So I never spent a lot of money on a record until I did Duran Duran's *Notorious*. Up until then, I did every record like a Black record – efficient, eight hours a day, that's it, done.

PLAN EVERY PENNY

Madonna was just starting out in her career when I started working with her on *Like a Virgin*. She used to say, "Time is money, and the money is mine". Which was great because that was how I produced. I'd say, "I know the money is yours, and I want to save it. The record company has given you an advance and you should be smart enough to make the record for as little as possible so you still have money to live off of until your royalties start streaming in."

OWN IT

As a creative person, the product you are making and selling is intellectual property (IP) so, as with any product, it's crucial that you make sure you own it. As many IP "products" are intangible rather than physical – e.g. music, movies, a logo, a screenplay – this can seem less obvious when you're starting out. In the beginning of Chic, we owned almost nothing we created. But we learned quickly – and the hard way. We were shocked to learn that other people owned what we'd created and were profiting from it – that we needed to own our creations.

The tough guys who'd loaned us $3,500 to make "Dance, Dance, Dance" wanted to keep the rights, while also taking all the credit for the hit, basically saying they'd discovered us on the street. Bernard and I had to split just 3 per cent, when we had a million-seller. Our contract said it was for one year, but we had made sure the contract specified that "the term one year shall henceforth be deemed six months". So they were forced to negotiate with us and we eventually got out of the contract and got our rights back.

So very soon after that, we made sure – in every negotiation and every contract – that we owned everything. Monetisation of our assets through owning the IP was key to survival in the ever-changing music business.

This point was really driven home to us while working with Diana Ross. To our surprise, we saw that she didn't own any of her work. So this major global superstar had to keep working for pay cheques, while we could have stopped and just lived off our royalties and licensing.

THE CENTRALITY OF CREATIVE COLLABORATIONS

As we all know, no one can do it alone and this is particularly true with creative enterprises – having great people around you is key. In my career, everything is about collaboration. I write for an ensemble: music to be performed by a group of people. I can play all the parts that I write, which is great because I understand them all completely. But I need other people to make my music come alive. When people work with me, they think that I'm the boss. But I always tell every artist I'm working with, "All you're doing is allowing me to join the band – for a month or two of your life, or even if it's just a day." The key to collaboration is trust. I try to make every artist understand that all I have is their best interest at heart. It's through these collaborations with people you trust and mutual support that you can achieve your goals.

THE IMPORTANCE OF BRAND PARTNERSHIPS

Especially in the beginning, associating your brand with another brand which is aligned and loved can be transformative. It can not only help expand your audience but also signal clearly and immediately what your brand is about, by association. For Chic, this was Studio 54. We basically started at the same time – "Dance, Dance, Dance" came out a few weeks after the club opened. The DJ from Studio 54 was a friend, and even though he didn't know anything about making records, we paid him to let us put his name on the record and say that it was mixed by him.

Because he was known as the Studio 54 DJ and Studio 54 was the centre of the disco universe, we knew that all the DJs around the world would see his name and go, "Wow, let's see what this is." And for us to be seen as part of the inner circle of Studio 54 was amazing. We couldn't go to the head of Studio 54 but we could go to the DJ. It was all about figuring out how you could get to the right people in the right way to get your brand associated in an audience's mind.

BEFORE THEY HEAR YOU, THEY SEE YOU

The look of your brand is crucial. I remember a very famous jazz musician who used to always dress impeccably. People would always ask him why he dressed like that when it was just going to make him sweaty and uncomfortable. His reply was something I live by to this day: "Before they hear you, they see you."

I heard this as a little kid. So when we were putting Chic together, and we were formulating the concept, that was in the front of my mind and a major influence on my seeing that the Roxy Music look was right for us and the importance of art direction. When we do our show now, when we walk out on stage that's a really big moment for people because they know we are going to wear something cool. A few days ago, I heard someone say, "I'd sure like to be in Nile's closet." Expressing your brand visually in every way is key.

THE FUNDAMENTALS: TRUST YOUR CORE VALUES, JUDGEMENT AND SKILLS

If you think something sounds logical, go with it. You have to know when something is right for you and is aligned with your values and brand. For example, in Chic's case, we received offers to produce The Rolling Stones, Barbara Streisand, Bette Middler – Dolly Parton even came to us. Everybody thought that we would just magically do a disco record for them. But that's just not who we were at all. You had to have the fundamentals in place, the background to know that Dolly Parton should not do a disco record, Dolly Parton should do an awesome country record that makes people want to dance to it, if I was going to do it! They believed that I had this sort of cookie cutter formula and I didn't.

I turned down Aretha Franklin, whom I think is amazing, because she wanted me to do a song she had written called "I'm going to be the only star tonight down at the disco." And I said, "Wait, they call you the Queen of Soul – how are you going to discard that moniker? If I'm going to work with you, I'm going to do the most soulful record I can think of; I'm not going to do a disco record." And she kind of fired me on the spot because I wouldn't do it.

The Business Plan

**Some semantic
and philosophical
preliminaries**

You hear all kinds of things about business plans: "You definitely need one, try to keep it down to 30 pages." "Do the financial forecasting for three to five years." "You don't need a business plan, they're a waste of time." "It doesn't make sense to have one, your business will change anyway." Why are there so many contradictory views? Because people are talking about different things in different contexts.

Mainstream discussions of business plans have become dominated by a particular model of business-building. Discussions often skip forwards, focusing on high-growth and fast-scaling businesses, without acknowledging that not all businesses are built the same.

The two topics covered in this book that are most subject to this presumption are **The Business Plan** and **Investors**. The assumed business-building model underlying discussions of these topics is a high-growth business that needs big investment early on in order to scale quickly, usually leading to an exit by the founder – either by going public, or by selling to a bigger company or private equity investor. This is the model for virtually all tech start-ups. You would be forgiven for thinking that a business plan is only one thing: a 30+ page document with a strict, standardised structure and extensive Excel spreadsheets of financial forecasting that only a Harvard MBA could produce.

Of course, there are some businesses like this in the creative sector, but the majority don't fall into this group. For example, in the UK, 95 per cent of creative companies are "micro-businesses" with fewer than 10 employees. This reflects the fact that creative people tend to think first about the creative idea and only later about making a business out of it; scaling and big revenue growth don't tend to be the leading factors. Just as we want to create a definition of "entrepreneur" that fits the creative sector, we also want to talk about "business plans" appropriately, and make clear the crucial distinctions between the different types.

This is the well-known Canvas Business Model Template

KEY PARTNERS

Are there any collaborations or partnerships that can help you enhance your creative business?

This could include working with other creatives, organisations, suppliers, or distributors.

KEY ACTIVITIES

What are the main activities involved in producing and delivering your creative work?

This could include designing, creating, marketing, and selling your artwork or services.

KEY RESOURCES

What resources do you need to create and deliver your creative products or services?

This could include artistic skills, materials, equipment, or access to distribution channels.

VALUE PROPOSITIONS

What unique value does your creative product or service offer to customers?

This could be innovative artwork, engaging storytelling, or unique experiences.

CUSTOMER RELATIONSHIPS

How will you interact with and engage your customers?

Will you provide personalised experiences, offer customer support, or build a community around your creative work?

CHANNELS

How will you reach your customers or audience?

Consider platforms such as social media, industry events, online marketplaces, or direct sales.

CUSTOMER SEGMENTS

Who are your target customers or audience?

Identify specific groups of people who would be interested in and willing to pay for your creative work. That could include individuals and businesses.

COST STRUCTURE

What are the main costs associated with running your creative business?

This could include materials, production costs, marketing expenses, or overhead costs like studio rent.

REVENUE STREAMS

How will you make money from your creative endeavors?

This could include selling work directly to consumers, brand partnerships, licensing your work, or hosting events.

A basic business plan

Let's start by saying that, no matter what, it really is important to have a plan. The key factor is not its form, but that it should address certain essential issues. As long as it does, it doesn't matter if it's on a single page, in a presentation or on the back of a napkin. The aim is to have a basic understanding of what the business will be and where it can go – and to think it through in a systematic way. This will serve as a key touchstone, helping you to organise your thoughts, stay true to your vision, prioritise your time and energy and measure progress as you go. The Canvas Business Model template on the previous page is a great format to help you create a basic plan.

Without this, you will almost certainly feel adrift and like you're just managing out of your inbox every day, rather than proactively driving your progress, true to your clearly defined vision. This inevitably leads to stress and sleepless nights. Not knowing how you will pay next month's rent is not conducive to creativity.

A business plan for high-growth businesses

This type of business plan has a set format that is expected by a range of stakeholders, including potential co-founders, investors, partners and key employees. It describes your business goals, strategies, operations, marketing and financial projections. It is an essential road map for the future, helping you clarify your initial business idea and objectives, avoid bumps in the road, and keep track of progress.

Even though this type of business plan is longer and more complex, it should be written by you, as a reflection of you. This is not a task to be delegated. It is a living, breathing document that will change over time as your business evolves; an essential home for all of your evolving plans and goals.

What to include

- **Executive summary** – a positive, engaging introduction to your business, condensed into one paragraph, that sets out what you are looking to achieve.
- **Business overview/background** – a general synopsis of the unmet need you are addressing with your business. What are the gaps in the market, what problems are you solving with your product/service, and how?
- **Product/service** – detail the key features and uniqueness of your product/service. What stage of development are you in? How will you get the product to the end market? Any visuals to include? (Further detail can sit in the appendix.)
- **Target market** – do your homework here, show your understanding of your potential audience, potential appeal, and your competitors. Are there any foreseeable market changes?
- **Marketing strategy and customer profile** – outline your sales, marketing and distribution strategies, and map your routes to market. What traction have you had to date? What are your customers' buying habits? How are you going to build a sales pipeline?
- **Operations** – this will vary depending on the business. No need to show a full process map but include key suppliers, team locations, any industry standards.
- **Management team** – the most important section for potential investors. Set out the business leaders, the team structure, and list their industry experience to date. (Full CVs can be included in the appendix.) Are there any non-executive directors or advisors to include?
- **Financial summary** – include 3-5 year forecasts and the rationale behind your predictions. Draw up profit and loss, cash flow, and a balance sheet.
- **Funding requirements** – how have you been financed to date? What is your investment requirement? Where will this take your company? Add valuation considerations.
- **Exit** – do you have an exit strategy? If so, how, why and when?

ROKSANDA ILINČIĆ

The Sculptress of Style

Roksanda Ilinčić

Founder of fashion label Roksanda

It is a summer evening in London in 2023 and Beyoncé is about to walk on stage to open the UK leg of her Renaissance tour – one of the most hotly anticipated and highest-grossing tours of all time.

As she appears, the crowd at Tottenham Hotspur Stadium goes wild – as does Roksanda Ilinčić and her team. Beyoncé is wearing the Yves Klein blue dress designed for her by Roksanda. Roksanda's team had been working with Beyoncé's team on the dress at breakneck speed for the past few weeks, but they had no idea she'd be wearing it on the opening night until they saw Mrs Carter appear on stage, at the same time as the 50,000 screaming stadium fans.

Not only was creating Beyoncé's headline look a major personal milestone for Roksanda as a designer, it took her business to new heights. Social media blew up, invaluable publicity ensued and sales soared – propelling the brand to new levels of conversation and influence.

Launching her brand in 2005 at London Fashion Week, Roksanda has become known for her sculptural aesthetic and striking use of colour blocking – more fine art than pure fashion. Her runway shows are legendary, set against iconic architectural backdrops such as the Serpentine Summer Pavilion and the brutalist icon Barbican Centre, and taking themes from seminal artists such as Dadaist sculptor-painter Jean Arp.

But as a highly talented creative entrepreneur, Roksanda has managed to bring her carefully crafted high art brand to the high street, striking up collaborations with favourite high street retailers such as Jigsaw – not to mention bringing it to Beyoncé's global audience.

I spoke to Roksanda at the Design Museum in London.

↗ Beyoncé on the opening night of her Renaissance Tour in London wearing Roksanda's custom Yves Klein Blue gown

↓ Roksanda Ilinčić: Highlights

- Born and raised in Serbia
- Studied architecture and design at the University of Arts Belgrade
- Earned a master's degree in 1999 from Central Saint Martins in London
- Launched Roksanda in 2005 at London Fashion Week
- Opened first store in Mount Street, Mayfair London in 2014
- British Fashion Awards "Red Carpet Award" (2012), *Harper's Bazaar* UK Women of the Year Awards "Business Woman of the Year" (2014), *Elle* Style Awards, "British Designer of the Year" (2016)
- Designs have been on display at the Design Museum and the V&A
- Clients include Catherine, Princess of Wales, Lady Gaga, Michelle Obama, Vanessa Redgrave, Cate Blanchett, Emily Blunt and Kristen Stewart
- Appointed Member of the Order of the British Empire (MBE) in 2023

London calling

I'm from Belgrade, Serbia, and from an early age I wanted to do fashion. I didn't quite recognise it as a profession, but it was something that I was always drawn to. I ended up studying Architecture and Applied Arts and part of this course was also fashion. I then applied to Central Saint Martins to do my masters.

I think London was to me, a young student from Belgrade, this incredible hub of experimentation, where there was freedom to push the boundaries of fashion. And I always wanted to be part of it. I felt that everything starts in London – particularly when it comes to fashion – and I wasn't wrong!

Roksanda, the brand, lifts off

After coming to London, I freelanced for different companies to earn money to start my own label. Once I had accumulated enough, I started very slowly with a tiny collection that only had 13 pieces. And that's how it all happened.

On the one hand, I didn't know what I was getting into. I think if I had known how hard it is, I would have probably been scared. But I think at a time when you've just graduated, when you're full of ideas that are your own and that you want to present to the world, there's something much stronger. Some inner voice inside of you that is pushing you to do the things you dream of.

TAKEAWAY | This is a great illustration of the value of following your instincts, even before you "know everything" – which you never will. While you want to do as much research as possible on how to make your business succeed, at a certain point, you need to make the judgement on when to dive in and start making it happen, so that you can start to get feedback and learn from there.

So I just kind of dove into this whole incredible world of fashion and somehow learned how to survive step by step, really very organically. I started out with a pure passion to do something that I felt strongly about, so had no business plan. But later, particularly with sponsorships, they ask for business plans, so that's when I started to make my first one.

Obviously now, I have a very strong business plan that I follow. It takes a lot of effort. It's like a big puzzle, and all the pieces have to work. You have to tick all the boxes and it's exciting and creative: how you approach certain problems, how you resolve them and how you approach your dreams and goals.

↖ Zendaya in Roksanda AW24
during the London press
tour for the *Dune: Part Two*

↑ Roksanda Ilinčić with *Bond*
actress Lashana Lynch,
wearing Roksanda at
the *Harper's Bazaar*
Women of the Year
Awards, London 2022

← Little Simz in Roksanda for
her *No Thank You* short film

The big breakthrough

My first breakthrough moment was when I showed in the official schedule at London Fashion Week in 2005. It was the moment when the buyers and the journalists (the people who really make a difference) came to see my show, and sensed that there was something interesting in it. It was then that the highly innovative and experimental department store Browns, run by the incredible Mrs B (legendary fashion retailer Joan Burstein), saw something in my designs immediately and took their chances to buy my collection and to stock me. After that, Harvey Nichols picked me up.

Going global

I think the designers in London have a lot of credibility globally. Once you are accepted in stores in London, the doors of every country begin to open. Then it's up to you to maintain those stockists and to grow with them, which is another step that is crucial, because once you manage to get into those stores you also have to maintain and grow the business. After getting these key stockists in London, people globally started to look at me as well. I started to get stockists all over the world and slowly, step by step, things started to happen.

TAKEAWAY   **It's so important to understand the process of building a business takes time. It's natural to feel impatient and not to understand why things take so long. But it's more important to take the pressure off of yourself and to get to grips with a realistic timescale – which you can do by comparing notes with all the friends and colleagues and mentors you can and by continuous research and learning. Holding yourself to an unrealistic timescale can be dangerous on so many levels, including compromising your business's success and your own wellbeing.**

And I think that is what helped me to find my way into this incredible business, as frankly I wasn't prepared at all – no matter how much inspiration I had or how different my designs were.

Taking the brand to the next level

My initial line has grown drastically. I now have pieces that cater for a woman's whole life – I often say 24 hours a day, seven days a week. It's from day to evening, it's knitwear, it's trousers, tops and dresses, separates, it's coats, it's everything.

It's important to create your style, to create your voice – something that is very recognisably you. And once you do that, it's important to follow it – to have a certain fundamental style

DNA that never changes. Collections change every season and you always have to come up with something new. I often challenge myself by incorporating things that I don't necessarily like to start with in order to add something fresh. But at the same time, my basic style constantly stays the same; it's very consistent.

TAKEAWAY **It can seem illogical, but consistency and innovation do not stand in opposition. It's crucial to have a consistent fundamental which defines your brand while at the same time creating completely new and original iterations as you go.**

 Because everything happened slowly, I had the opportunity to learn everything I could from my own mistakes and those of others.

Social media has also been a big step forward, as it is great for understanding the market but also presenting your voice. That didn't exist when I started. Instagram is a great platform that's allowing everybody, no matter where they live, to show their work. To be able to reach your audience directly and have this ongoing relationship with them is a different world.

→ Roksanda Ilinčić after winning the inaugural award for Best Red Carpet Designer at the *Elle* Style Awards in 2013

→ Roksanda Ilinčić returning to the *Elle* Style Awards in 2016, winning British Designer of the Year

Two big leaps forward, investment and my first shop

For my brand, the first big leap forward was getting financial backing. Initially, that came from sponsorship schemes through the British Fashion Council. After that, I got equity investment from an investor.

I was lucky enough to find an investor who was doing things from the heart with a big passion for fashion. They had an understanding as a consumer, and came from the perspective of somebody who is probably as obsessed with fashion as I am! At that stage, that was a perfect choice and a perfect partner to have. But finding the right investor is a big challenge, so I consider myself very lucky.

TAKEAWAY

Not all businesses or founders are suited to investors, but if you are sure you want one, the most important thing is to make sure that they totally understand your brand, your goals and your values. It's like getting married, not something to be taken lightly.

Getting that investment let me open my first store: my second big leap forward. It allowed me to present an immersive window into my whole world. I collaborated with architect David Adjaye to design the store. It wasn't just about the clothes; it was also the smell when you walk through the door, the way the shop is constructed, the colours that we use in the store, how it makes you feel. It was a step forward not just into the world of fashion, but into the world of Roksanda.

Investment allowed me to fulfil my dreams of making the store as beautiful as it is now, and also to expand the business drastically – starting with employing two new staff. I extended my ranges which are now much bigger than before, the biggest addition being accessories, including my bag range.

↗ Roksanda AW22 Runway
   at the Tate Britain,
   London Fashion Week,
   February 2022

↪ Roksanda AW20 Runway
   at the Foreign &
   Commonwealth Office,
   London Fashion Week,
   February 2020

↓ Passing on lessons learned

LEARN QUICKLY OR BE REPLACED
If you don't learn quickly enough in fashion, someone will take your place. You don't have a choice. I had to adapt quickly at the beginning, it's a matter of survival. That's an entrepreneurial approach.

STRIKING THE BALANCE BETWEEN CREATIVITY AND COMMERCE
What is important in sustaining a creative business is that you have this incredible creative vision that should lead everything and not be undermined, but at the same time you have to be pragmatic. At the end of the day, clothes need to be worn and need to be loved by women, not only by galleries. I think that it's important to understand that and to build a business so that it's constantly growing and conquering new territories and new customers, rather than creating something that is just for beauty alone.

ALWAYS SPEAK TO YOUR CUSTOMER
You have to create a product that talks to people. It's important that it's not just about the dress, not just about another skirt; it's about certain emotions that people get when wearing these clothes – something like falling in love. I was lucky enough to create dresses that women recognised, and that had a certain conversation with them and made them feel empowered.

OVERCOMING CHALLENGES
We all have doubts, and bad days and good days. There were many moments when I doubted myself, as I tend to be my own worst critic. Particularly in the beginning, it's very hard to have your voice heard and to get the support that you need so much. There were moments then when I wanted to give up. But I was lucky that, over time, I'd built relationships with great people and at the times when I needed support the most, they came through to help me.

CREATIVE BOUNDARIES
My biggest lesson was how to control my creativity. When you graduate, you haven't set your own creative boundaries and sometimes you go too much in one direction and not enough in another. Getting the balance right was the best thing for me, and something that took a long time.

NAVIGATING THE PRODUCTION PROCESS
The production process can be quite challenging for designers at the beginning, because you have to pay for everything upfront, from fabrics and pattern cutters to factories, and then deliver to the stockists. They can pay within one or two months, depending on what the deal is, so you have to put up quite a lot of money upfront. It is what it is, and you just have to find your way around it and build a system for yourself that is sustainable.

THE IMPORTANCE OF MENTORS
Mentors make all the difference. One who was crucial for me, among many many others, was a great teacher at Central Saint Martins called Louise Wilson. She was a mentor not just in terms of creativity and design, but also in terms of business. She had a very harsh way of saying the truth straight to your face; something I think you need at that stage. I really looked up to her and collected all her advice. Without her guidance, I wouldn't have been able to have such a strong point of view from the beginning.

SUCCESS TAKES TIME AND RELENTLESSNESS

Sales didn't happen overnight. You need to understand your customer and to educate them to get used to your designs, it takes time. I remember Yasmin Sewell, a buyer at Browns, and also Mrs B, saying to me, "Listen, we didn't sell out of your things, but we believe in you. So, together we will reach good results, if not this first season, then in the next couple of seasons." And that's exactly what happened, and I'm still with them. I'm one of the brands that they never dropped.

A drive to push yourself always has to be there, you can never rest, it's relentless. That's the nature of fashion, and something I didn't really expect.

WORK/LIFE BALANCE

You find a way to make it work. In my case, I thought that the most important thing in the world was fashion. But after having my daughter I realised that it's not so! I think it's great to have that balance of really hard work and a really beautiful personal life.

FIND YOUR WAY

I think we are all different and we all come from different backgrounds and have a different plot twist to start from. Everybody has to find their own path. I think that I followed a particular path which was quite hard. I must say it's quite slow, but it's certainly very rewarding as well. Follow your instincts and your own gut. Don't listen to too many advisors at the beginning.

ENJOY THE JOURNEY

It's very much about the journey as well and if you are not enjoying it, then it might not be the right path for you.

HIRE WELL

It was important for me to hire a team that could help on the operations side of the business, so that my time could be spent being creative. Of course, I'm involved in all aspects of the business, but it's almost impossible to move forward without having this type of support – so finding the right team is crucial.

LEARN HOW TO DELEGATE

This was definitely something that I needed to work on. It wasn't easy to let things go, and I probably still find it hard these days! But it's something that you need to conquer in order to grow. Because, unfortunately, we are not able to clone ourselves and we are not able to do everything ourselves. We need to delegate, and if you have the right people around you then it's actually not as hard as it seems at the beginning.

Building Your Brand

Your brand is your everything, especially in the creative sector. It's your business's DNA: how every person experiences your business at every touchpoint. It's you, your vision, your golden goose.

Why "especially in the creative sector"? Because people generally buy a creative product or service due to an emotional connection, because it's the product of your imagination that speaks to someone else's. The feeling that a brand evokes is essential to its success.

Let's have a closer look.

What is a brand?

Broken down, a brand is a set of values, experiences, associations and knowledge connected with a product, service or company. It's the perception of your business by the outside world, and it's what sets you apart from the competition. Most of all, building a stand-out brand leads to the Holy Grail of any business: customer loyalty. That long-term relationship helps you achieve dependable repeat sales, word-of-mouth recommendations and the ability to experiment and raise prices.

Brand Loyalty

More loyalty results in customers being more likely to make future purchases.

Also boosts your ability to increase prices without losing customers Loyal customers are also more likely to recommend you brand, and help spread awareness.

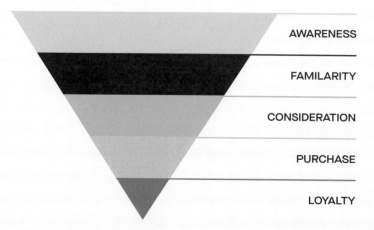

AWARENESS

FAMILARITY

CONSIDERATION

PURCHASE

LOYALTY

Branding vs. marketing

Branding is who you are as a business and where you sit in your market.

Marketing, on the other hand, is how you get your brand out into the world and tell your brand story.

How to build a brand

First, define your USP

What basic human value does your business offer? Is it freedom, empowerment, expression, connection or something else?

How is the way you work different? Do you offer something more sustainable, efficient or beautiful? Is there a cause you support/champion?

Next, define your brand DNA

Including your conclusions above, work out who you are as a business, broken down into your:
- **Mission:** Your "why" – your purpose, intention and overall objectives. Why do we exist, and what do we contribute to the world?
- **Vision:** A mental image of what your business will look like when it achieves its goals
- **Values:** The principles that guide and direct your business and its culture

Define your brand position: identify your target audience

Who: target audience? You may find you have more than one target audience – that's fine
What: brands and products they buy and aspire to?
When: do they make purchasing decisions?
Where: do they purchase and use products like yours?
Why: what are the drivers and barriers to their purchases?

Brand Pyramid

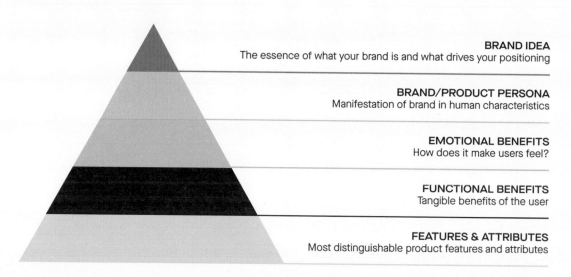

BRAND IDEA
The essence of what your brand is and what drives your positioning

BRAND/PRODUCT PERSONA
Manifestation of brand in human characteristics

EMOTIONAL BENEFITS
How does it make users feel?

FUNCTIONAL BENEFITS
Tangible benefits of the user

FEATURES & ATTRIBUTES
Most distinguishable product features and attributes

Define your brand position: identify your competitors

Who are your key competitors?
What sorts of language and imagery do they use?
Where (digital and in person) do they place their brands?
How would you characterise their customers?
How does your brand differ?

Check out competitor websites and social media channels and visit their stores. Collect as much of their marketing material as possible; take pictures of packaging, signage and products. You could also interview consumers in the market about their brand perceptions and preferences.

Create your brand story

Your brand story builds on, and encapsulates, all the elements above to create a simple, compelling narrative of your business's origins, mission and purpose. It lets you create an emotional connection with your customers and is often told in the voice of the founder. This story will be a cornerstone of your brand, and you will want to revisit and update it over time as your brand evolves.

Prepare your "brand assets"

These are the tools you should create to communicate your brand story to the outside world.
- Visual assets:
  → These include your logo, typeface, brand colours and the types of images and formats you use
  → Use visual cues to suggest the abstract ideas behind your brand story. Test your visual identity on friends and family – do they communicate your brand story clearly?

- Written assets – these include: Your company description in different lengths:
  → Tag line
  → Elevator pitch (description in one minute)
  → Brief overall summary of the company
  → A statement of your **mission, vision, values and USP**

- Your brand **tone of voice.** This is generally for internal use to keep you and your team in alignment with your brand story. This isn't what your brand says, but how it says it.

Bring your brand assets to life through key formats including

- Printed material such as business cards, packaging, signage, etc.
- Digital content including your website, social media platforms, advertising, videos and any apps
- Original content – for example, a company newsletter, blogs, interviews and collaborations

Final thoughts...
Remember to bring your team along with you: they are your brand ambassadors and convey the brand culture you are creating. And make your top priority building an amazing experience for your customers at every point, giving you the best chance to earn their valuable loyalty.

YINKA ILORI

The Architect of Joy

Yinka Ilori

Founder of Yinka Ilori Studio

Yinka Ilori realised he'd reached a turning point. It was 2015 and he was completely frustrated with the whole design industry. He'd started his own practice designing furniture, primarily chairs ("Everyone called me 'The Chairman'"), and after four years was struggling to get it off the ground. His concept was to turn discarded chairs, which he would find on the street, into sculptural pieces which could tell stories drawing on his Nigerian-British heritage. He felt that people took chairs somewhat for granted, while they're actually quite powerful, as they unite people – we sit on a chair to tell stories, to celebrate, to relax, to argue, to sing, to spend time with our loved ones, to signal hierarchy.

But instead of picking up on the stories he was trying to tell, he felt everyone just reduced him to a label – artist, designer, marketer. He was struggling to break into galleries and design weeks and to get stocked at major British design stores like Habitat and Heal's. He saw that they had their favourites and were unwilling to think outside the box. To make matters worse, he wasn't making any money – in fact, his practice was costing him money. So he made a plan to quit design.

Before he did – out of pure frustration and because he had nothing left to lose – he decided to design his own collection of chairs. He would tell his own purely authentic, unfiltered story – not the diluted stories he realised he'd been telling until then, which he felt pressured to tell to make them easier for people to swallow and to get press. For this purely personal collection, he wouldn't contact any PR people; instead he wrote his own press release and commissioned his own photographer. He called his collection *If Chairs Could Talk*.

Yinka was working at Jigsaw (a major British fashion chain) at the time and had told them he was an artist. When they asked to see his work he showed them his collection. They were impressed. As it happened, Jigsaw also owned The Shop at Bluebird in the King's Road, a high profile design-led concept store featuring cutting-edge fashion and contemporary design. One thing led to

↗ *The Flamboyance of Flamingos* playground in London by Yinka Ilori

↓ Yinka Ilori: Highlights

- Born and raised in London to Nigerian parents
- Graduated from London Metropolitan University in Furniture Design
- Breakthrough project: *If Chairs Could Talk* 2015, a collection of upcycled chairs
- *The New York Times* "One of 12 Talents Shaping the Design World"
- Canary Wharf "Creative Courts" kaleidoscopic basketball court
- Dulwich Picture Gallery "Colour Palace"

- Designed The British Fashion Awards Trophy 2022
- Collaborations with Courvoisier, Lego, M&S, Bulgari, Selfridges, Browns
- Exhibited at MoMA, Design Museum, V&A, Guggenheim Bilbao, Vitra
- *Architectural Digest* AD 100 2024
- Honoured by Queen Elizabeth II with an MBE for contributions to design

another, and Yinka got an email from Bluebird saying they wanted to put on a show for his collection at the store. That show put him on the map and changed his life.

If Chairs Could Talk became a hit at the prestigious London Design Festival. The Brighton Museum then acquired one of the chairs. A few years later, the world-leading, Frank Gehry-designed Vitra Design Museum in Basel acquired another for their Making Africa exhibition, which toured the world, including the Guggenheim Bilbao and the Whitney Museum in New York. A few years later, The Metropolitan Museum of Art (the Met) and the Victoria and Albert Museum (V&A), both of which are in their permanent collections.

Yinka has now expanded to become a multidisciplinary artist, architect and designer of joy. He's turned his hand (and his heart) to public spaces including children's playgrounds and murals, homewares (releasing a collection at the MoMA Design Store in New York), fashion and product design for Courvoisier and Bulgari, as well as designing the trophies for the BRIT Music Awards and the London Fashion Awards. His unique visual language of dazzling colours and playful design draws on his Nigerian-British heritage and his passion for bringing people together and telling stories.

I spoke to Yinka at his Yinka Ilori Studio in West London.

The beginning

My parents grew up in Nigeria and came to London, where I was born, in the 1980s. They're very traditional Nigerian parents and wanted me to be an engineer, doctor or scientist, to make sure I'd have a guaranteed income and stability, which is understandable. I must have been so annoying saying, "I want to be a designer, I want to tell stories." But I did have the impression that most fine artists only made money after they died, which put me off studying fine art. Instead, I studied furniture design at London Metropolitan University, because I thought it seemed more tangible – more about actual products.

A perspective from today

From starting my career, it took me about 15 years to finally say, "I'm an artist, I'm not starving, I'm actually making a living out of this." But it is hard – there's no manual to show you how to do it and what the bumps might be. You just have to kind of go with the flow.

A key factor is having the right people around you. For me, one of the first was Lee Broom, a leading product designer in East London. I interned with him for about six months after I finished my

↑ From *If Chairs Could Talk*
Yinka's breakthrough
exhibition at Bluebird,
King's Road, London

↗↘*There is Good in All of Us*
exhibition commissioned by
fashion brand MCM

graduate degree. That was absolutely key because he gave me my first insights into running a design studio; how to actually run a business. When you're an artist, you can forget it's also a business. He's a creative, but I saw first-hand how he was running a business – running and paying a team, paying taxes, etc. These are things you have to consider, but that creative people tend not to have a background in.

↓ "Oorun Didun" (Nigerian for "sweet sun"), Yinka's first homeware collection, designed in collaboration with New York's iconic Museum of Modern Art (MoMA)

There's no manual

No one tells you how to structure your business, whether you should set up a company or just do business as an individual person (known as a "sole trader" in the UK or a "sole proprietorship" in the US), and what the pros and cons are. Or about filing your sales tax ("VAT" in the UK, "sales tax" in the US) returns. Or about making sure to set money aside to pay taxes at the end of the tax year. I was stunned when I first set up my company, because I spent and spent and spent during the first year, and when it came time to pay the company taxes, I didn't have the money. You learn from your mistakes in these areas, but there's certainly no manual.

Artists just want to create; they don't really care about the numbers. So I always try to share with younger creatives, asking them: *Hey, what's that contract you're signing, how long is it for? Do you own your IP?* What are the terms, what's the royalty? Because I've been there before. It's about sharing knowledge with up-and-coming creatives. It's about how they can be a creative, but also run a business, because that piece is crucial – it's a long game.

Longevity is the key

I always think about longevity: how do you keep going and reinvent yourself?

> You can do too much too soon and you can go bust if you don't manage your money properly.

You see it in a lot of studios that go really big quickly, but there's no strategy, and they just go under. For example, a design studio can spend a lot of money just putting together a bid – if they don't get the job and they keep doing that, they're going to fold, as they can't sustain it.

You've got to have a strategy, a business plan, and artists don't think about that at all. I try to diversify what we do in the studio – we work across architecture, set design, homewares, objects that are meaningful and story-led based on my personal experience and heritage, and also a lot of fashion. So it's about how you can find diversified areas to work in and also diversified revenue streams. For example, for us, aside from individual commissions, brand collaborations are key.

| TAKEAWAY | It's crucial to have a long-term plan for your business. It doesn't have to be complicated in the beginning, you just need to be clear on some key basics. For example, what is your strategy on spending, what are you getting long-term for money you plan to spend? Are the amounts sustainable? Where do you see your revenue coming from? Can you identify additional revenue streams from different areas of work you might be able to engage in? Are these revenue streams sustainable long-term? |

People like Damien Hirst, Jeff Koons or Anish Kapoor sell works for millions of dollars, but that's very rare and it takes a long time to get to that position. Creative people need to understand that.

Your people are key

People are such a big part of my journey and my story, they've helped me so much. I didn't have any formal business advice starting out, I just listened to people around me. Yinka Shonibari (the multi-award-winning artist) coached me on managing money. He also invests his own money in giving back – for example, through his art residency and community in Nigeria, then bringing those artists to London for exposure and cultural exchange.

Fashion designer Oswald Boetang has also been like a mentor to me, always giving me business advice. Just a couple of weeks ago, Oswald was talking to me about longevity. His fashion business has been around for about 30 years, and he's the only Black person on Saville Row. To be there for that long is amazing. He's a prime example of how you keep going, how you reinvent yourself: yes he's creative, but how do you sustain that business?

The beauty of slow growth

I grow my team quite slowly. There are about 15 of us in the studio now, a mixture of employees and freelancers. I never wanted to scale my business – the financial burden of having to be responsible for people's mortgages and other responsibilities scares me. Money management comes into it, because you can get all of this work coming in and then, for reasons out of your control (the economy, a recession), work can run dry and then you can't afford everything.

→ "Laundrette of Dreams" interactive art installation and play space to imagine how play can make the most mundane routines joyful, London

I like slow growth. It lets you control where your brand goes and how you want to live your life. My work is so personal, it's coming from me, from my family, so it's hard for my team to start any project without my deep personal involvement. I kind of feel like I'm a con if I don't give the client "me". It comes from

somewhere personal and then my team develops it. So, the idea of having a CEO just doesn't work for me. I've got a great team and a great project manager, great mentors and agents. That's enough for me.

You've got to understand what you really want, because you can get pushed into something you don't want to go into. Someone can have a vision for you and say: "You need to go here", and you can get carried away and then you get there, and you're like: "I just don't really want this." It's been very important to me to be clear on my own vision and what I want to do.

 I like intimate spaces, I like an intimate team; from budgets to production, I know everyone who helps us or produces for us, so that's something I want to maintain for as long as I'm here.

Investors

I've considered investors, but I don't want the burden that comes with it: the lack of control you then have and the obligation to pay money back. I've seen people who've gotten investors who then kick them out, or fold the company because it hasn't done what it needed to do in their eyes. And you've lost all your hard work because someone else who runs your company makes those decisions – it's a very hard thing to see. I think a lot of people just think it's great to get investment money in the door and don't realise the very serious risks involved.

TAKEAWAY A simple but important point to recognise: investors will want their money back, in multiples, at some point. And they will require ownership in your company, which will give them a level of control, depending on what percentage of your company's shares you give them. While the right investor can be a huge help, and ideally a partner to you in growing your business, it's very important to understand the corresponding obligations you are taking on, especially in the beginning when it's important to have time to experiment before being locked in to a rigid business plan, which investors normally require.

Building your brand and working with others

I'm building my own brand. That's why brands like Courvoisier or Bulgari want to work with me: they want to connect to my story, which is about joy in public spaces and in art and design. But the business side has to come into it as well.

For example, I rent my studio space in West London, which is expensive – it costs more than the mortgage on my home. Thinking long-term about the business, I'm considering investing in studio space which I can own, so I get the long-term economic growth but can also offer space to other artists at affordable rents. And it would also help the general community, because creatives are so important to our society – they bring beauty and joy.

Again, what's the strategy? I can't do that now, but I'm constantly re-evaluating when I can do it, depending on the money coming in. Also this is a new generation of wealth, coming from my generation. Revenue models are changing in the creative sector and it's very different now. For example, look at the music industry, with streaming, which has changed the business model completely. So it's about thinking, *How does my generation stay on top of these trends and invest to assure longevity?*

| TAKEAWAY | While being immersed in the day-to-day of your business, it's easy to lose track of the bigger picture and longer term. Keep a note or make a mood board of your bigger picture goals, and come back to it regularly so you can continue to evaluate how and when you can progress your longer term goals.

A crucial early start from The Prince's Trust

The Prince's Trust helped me a lot with my business plan. They're probably the reason I'm actually here. I had a mentor there who helped me write my business plan about how to start my studio. I pitched it to others within Prince's Trust, like *Dragon's Den*. I pitched my idea about upcycling furniture and storytelling and I got a £3,500 loan to start my studio. Another mentor there [Lawrence Colbert] worked at Virgin, and he commissioned me to design a sofa for his office which he still has now – he changed my life.

Collaborating and telling new stories

Any project is better when you collaborate because you get new and old influences and ideas. For example, LionHeart [an award-winning poet] and Thomas Heatherwick worked together on Thomas's "Tree of Trees" for King Charles' Coronation. Thomas has been in business for 30 years, LionHeart for only a few years. It's unexpected and exciting, as people think they come from different worlds. It shows the power of art and design, that you share an idea and emotion and that brings us together.

I think what's interesting now is that my generation of artists are telling different stories, stories that previous generations probably weren't able to tell when they were starting out because people may not have understood those narratives. For example, I'm talking about stories from Nigerian culture, the folklore and wisdom – older generations probably didn't feel they could express themselves in that way.

But for the newer generations, there's such an emphasis on telling authentic stories and controlling the narrative themselves versus having their stories controlled, or even dismissed, by gatekeepers. Social media is a key channel for this, helping people reach audiences directly.

Social media has changed the game

Social media has changed everything.

> For example, art galleries having to say, "I'll give you a show." Well, no, I can have a show on Instagram.

I can share my opinions, share my ideas and create my own community on Instagram. I think it makes the creative space so much more accessible and inclusive, and global. I can DM someone in LA, they might reply to me or not, but I can get to them directly. That's the beauty of social media – at the tip of your fingers you can put work and ideas and requests out there.

↗ Limited-edition
  Courvoisier VSOP Cognac
  bottle and Pop-Up
  Courvoisier Lounge at
  Selfridges, London
  designed by Yinka Ilori

↑ Collaboration with the
  Bulgari Hotel in London

→ Trophy for The British
  Fashion Awards 2022
  designed by Yinka Ilori

↓ Passing on lessons learned

CONSTANTLY REEVALUATE YOUR STRATEGY

I'm still trying to work out the business side of things, the strategy. For example, the homeware side of the business, called "My Objects", will hopefully be ticking away self-sufficiently on its own. I can scale that: I design the pieces and they can be mass produced, without losing my personal touch. That provides steady revenue which opens up space for me to do my own passion projects. It means I don't have to rely on brands to let me do those projects, which is great because I'm trying to create my own brand. It's a virtuous circle, as my passion projects help build my brand but also make my work for brands and my mass-produced objects more attractive.

THE ART OF WORKING WITH BRANDS

I love working with brands – the right brands who are aligned with mine. It lets you tap into new audiences that you couldn't reach on your own and elevate your own brand.

For example, major British retailer Marks & Spencer [specialising in food, fashion and home products] asked me to design a version of their famous shopping bag. I'd been doing a few bags for a long time, but not on the scale I could do with M&S. It was just a simple bag we put food in, that we all use, and it went international. I'm always banging on about how good design should be accessible, totally contrary to this whole idea that art needs to cost millions – no! And that M&S bag proved it. I get emails from people from around the world just to say, "I bought your bag, I'm in Brazil, I bought ten for my family" or, "I'm Nigerian and I bought the bag

because I saw that you're Nigerian. I have a mixed race daughter and I wanted to inspire her that she can be an artist, she can be successful, because you did it."

It's those emails that make me feel like what I'm doing makes sense and it's needed and it's touching people and I need to continue. My mission is always to create objects that are accessible. For example, people of my parents' generation don't want to go to an art gallery, but they do want to invest 15 pence in a bag that's signed by an artist – for me that's enough. It's a 360-degree experience for me, as I used to work at M&S – it has so many touch points in my life.

STAY TRUE TO YOUR OWN BRAND WHILE WORKING WITH OTHERS

You have to be thinking about how you keep the business going, but always staying authentic and true to your values. Sometimes you work with a brand and it's soulless. You can do it for the money, but it doesn't elevate you to the next level or open a new door, which can prove to be an opportunity cost in the long run. So, I always think strategically. I want to get into that space; if I work on this project, will it get me into that space? If it does, then yeah, I'll do it. It's always about the creativity, of course, but also about the business, about the plan.

Brands I work with have always let me be myself because I've worked hard over the years to make clear what my work is about. It's obvious to them what they'll get from me – I'm going to give joy. So, for a brand it's great, because they know what's coming. I'm going to 1) tell their story; 2) give it a sense of joy; 3) connect their brand with something new they've never experienced before; and 4) create a memory that will live in that brand's heart and that they can share with people forever. Those are the pillars of what I try to bring out on each project.

FIND YOUR DISTINCTIVE VOICE

After working very hard over many years, my style has become distinctive, I don't have to speak; you know it's me when you see it, you know it's my work and where it's coming from. I think I've been able to carve out that design language authentically – it's something I haven't forced, it's just kind of happened. I've found joy and my voice, and joy within my work, and it's my USP. You can design a visual language that people can connect with. I want my work to inspire emotion where you're smiling – you're not thinking about smiling, you're just smiling. We don't do enough of that and that's why my language is so powerful; it can really evoke emotion.

I think design and art can play a role in connecting with emotions, like medicine in a way.

WORKING WITH NATURE

My next big focus is nature. Before there was architecture, there was nature. How do we benefit from it? I really connected with nature during the pandemic, with trees and birds and water – these powers that are in nature, the miracle of the seasons, are things we often don't stop and notice. I was probably my best self during those two years and put out some of my best work. It gave me space to think and also let me go back to my childhood and remember experiencing the different emotions and feelings when I was outside and what it did for me. It's so important to connect with what's at your core, to remember what's always inspired you and to make time for that.

Intellectual Property

IP: Everything you need to know

What is IP?

Intellectual property (IP) protects the "fruits" of creativity and inventiveness. It describes a collection of intangible assets or rights, including patents, trademarks and copyright. These assets are particularly relevant to creative entrepreneurs, as they are selling just that – the fruits of creativity.

IP is all about giving you exclusive control over your creative work, inventions or brand assets. This right prevents other people from copying, commercialising or using them.

But while IP protects the expression, fixation or manifestation of an idea or concept, it doesn't generally protect ideas or concepts in their abstract sense.

Although it's not physical, IP is just as valuable:

It can be:
- bought and sold (aka "assigned")
- rented (aka "licensed" or "granted")
- given as security for a debt
- given as security for an investment

IP rights can be categorised in different ways

By their ability to be registered:
- Trademarks, patents and registered designs are registered rights – and you have to actively apply for them
- Copyright and confidential information are unregistered (or non-registrable) rights, which arise automatically – but you can put a contract in place to protect them

By the subject matter they cover:
- Brands are protected by trademarks, copyright and design rights
- Products may be protected by copyright, design rights and patents
- Information may be protected by confidentiality, data and database rights

Protecting your brand

A trademark is a mark or sign that indicates the origin of your product or service, so your customers can easily identify your brand. Examples of trademarks are: words, slogans, logos, shapes, colours, sounds or even smells.

3 things to ask yourself:

Which marks do you need to protect?

Make your trademark distinctive (not descriptive) – lots of famous brands have distinctive trademark names (which include no mention of the goods or services they relate to), e.g. Starbucks, Google, Uber, McDonald's. Don't use your trademark to tell your consumers what to do. It's a good idea to conduct trademark searches in advance before you file yours. As well as being distinctive, your trademark needs to be recognisable as a trademark. And it needs to be original...

Which products/services do you need to protect?

Give some careful thought to which different classes of goods or services to include in your trademark application. If you expand your business in the future, you won't be able to extend the classes retrospectively (you'd need to reapply). This could be a problem a few years down the line and could potentially prevent your business's expansion. Say you're currently selling clothing, footwear and headgear, but in five to ten years you'll want to start selling sunglasses, bags and jewellery. It's a good idea to include those additional classes of goods and services in your application now. Otherwise, someone else could claim the same or similar trademark for the classes you'll need.

Which countries or territories do you need to cover?

If you want to file your trademark in several different countries or territories, you'll need to do this separately for each one (there are some exceptions to this rule, including in the EU, where one application can cover all 27 member states, and in the US, where one application covers all 50 states).

Final word on trademarks...

Use them or lose them: Trademarks can last forever, but you do need to renew them every 10 years. Also, you need to use and maintain them, otherwise they can be cancelled after three to five years. It might be wise to keep evidence of your usage in case someone challenges your trademark. You should expect copycats and infringers, so be ready to assert your rights. Take advice and have an enforcement strategy in place.

Protecting your products and materials

You have three "rights" to protect you:
- **Copyright**: Copyright covers a broad range of original creative works, including literary and artistic works, video/audio recordings and software. It also covers advertising and marketing materials, social media, trade materials, etc. It's a very useful and flexible right.
- **Design rights**: Design rights protect the shape, configuration and aesthetics of new designs, e.g. if you design new or distinctive-looking clothing, footwear, furniture, toys, bags or jewellery, etc. You can use your design rights to exercise control and prevent people from copying you.
- **Patents**: Patents protect new inventions such as a new, inventive and non-obvious next step, product, process or solution. Patents are common in the gaming, technology and pharmaceutical industries. They're expensive and can be time-consuming to acquire.

Copyright and design rights are probably more relevant to your start-up creative business than patents.

Protecting your information

Information can be hugely valuable:
- Identify all your valuable confidential information (sensitive material like trade secrets, internal know-how, private processes and methodologies, etc.) and use non-disclosure agreements (NDAs) to keep it out of the public domain
- Identify all your valuable databases or datasets and control them by applying copyright rules, e.g. make sure you have the right contracts in place
- Comply with any regulatory obligations around customers' personal data, e.g. GDPR in Europe and equivalent regulations in other countries

C '

You keep your five hundred dollars,
and I'll keep the copyright.

Jo March to her publisher
in Greta Gerwig's *Little Women*

C

ANDY HARRIES

The Crown King of TV & Film

Andy Harries

Founder of Left Bank Pictures

There was television – and then there was *The Crown*. A watershed phenomenon that has transformed the art form as we know it. Not a TV series in the traditional sense, *The Crown* is essentially a series of theatrical films, each with the accompanying rich cinematic production values, lavish budgets and meticulous research.

It has also reinvented a genre of storytelling. Following a family drama over decades, it has, for the first time, changed cast members every two of its six seasons, rejecting the standard practice of "ageing" the same cast members over the life of a series. And, most controversially, portrayed real-life events of the world's most famous and most private family in documentary style, while filling in the blanks with conversations and feelings imagined by genius writer Peter Morgan.

The Crown is one of the most successful, influential, beloved and argued-over creations in television history. Netflix commissioned the show in 2016 – the streaming site's first original content commission – and it has since become the platform's biggest hit. There were many moments of alchemy that brought *The Crown* to life, but here is one. As a TV producer at Granada Television, Andy Harries had convinced Helen Mirren to reprise her role in *Prime Suspect*, an iconic British psychological detective drama, which was a vehicle to tell bigger stories about society and politics. At a *Prime Suspect* cast and crew read-through in London, everyone was gathered and waiting for Helen. When she swept into the room, Andy noticed something. "People sort of bowed to her," he remembers, "almost collapsing in front of her. I thought *My God, she's like the Queen!* A bell went off in my head. I rushed up to her and said, 'Have you ever thought about playing the Queen?' She looked at me as if I was crazy but admitted that it wasn't the first time she'd heard the comparison."

"I got Stephen Frears [award-winning director of *My Beautiful Laundrette*, *Dangerous Liaisons* and *The Grifters*] on speed dial and said, 'I'm with Helen Mirren and I've just had this crazy idea about working with her on a film about the Queen.' Stephen said, in his one-and-only distinctive way, 'Oh that's a good

↗ Claire Foy (the young Queen
  Elizabeth) and Matt Smith
  (the young Prince Philip)
  in *The Crown*, 2017

↓ Andy Harries: Highlights

- One of the most successful and celebrated producers of TV and film today
- Founder of Left Bank Pictures, whose productions are based on quintessentially British content, made for a global audience
- Started his career as a journalist

- Producer of Oscar-winning *The Queen* and Multiple Emmy- and BAFTA-winning *The Crown*
- Other creative highlights: *The Jonathan Ross Show*, *The Royle Family*, *Cold Feet*, *Prime Suspect*

idea.' So, I connected them immediately to keep the momentum going. Then I rang Peter Morgan. Peter's contribution was enormous because he found the structure and brought the story to life, dramatising it beautifully. *The Queen* was huge for Peter and me – and for Helen, who won the Oscar. It changed everything. And, of course, although we didn't know it at the time, it was a precursor to *The Crown*."

I spoke to Andy at Left Bank Pictures in London.

Stirrings of the imagination

I remember sitting in the cinema as a young child, dazzled by the movies and thinking it would be fantastic to be involved in them somehow – but never envisioning I could. My first job when I left school at 17 was working as a junior reporter for the *Evening Telegraph* in Peterborough. I did this for a year and loved it, imagining travelling the world as a foreign correspondent.

I went to University of Hull and studied politics. After graduating, I briefly went back into newspapers, but I found that my journalistic career had become quite radicalised. My political views were very left of centre – and the seventies were troubled times with the collapse of the Labour government and the miners' strikes. So, finding journalism no longer quite fitted, I applied for other jobs and accepted a role at Granada Television in Manchester, writing the trailers. Granada at that time was a fantastic independent TV company, famous for its entertainment, dramas and shows like *World in Action* – an investigative journalists' programme which broke big global stories. At age 21, I liked that Granada was far from London, culturally left of centre and "anti-establishment".

 We were encouraged to break the rules and to see television as a way to experiment and agitate a bit.

TAKEAWAY

This is a great illustration of the importance, in the early stages of your career, of following your passions and interests – what you're drawn to and feel you excel at. They may feel all over the place and slightly random, but they end up shaping you in ways you'll later see and will also form a cohesive whole once you have enough distance to look back at them with perspective.

The importance of failing

The natural evolution from being a researcher is to be a producer. The system required that I pass a particular exam for producers. Much to my frustration, I failed it not once but three times at Granada. When I failed my third exam at age 26, I was devastated. The executive producer said, "You know, Andy, we just don't think you're cut out for television." I was shell-shocked – but nothing has ever provided more rocket fuel for my ambition than those words.

TAKEAWAY

Everyone hates failure. But as Andy puts it, it can serve as powerful rocket fuel, energising you to clarify your goals and giving you something to fight for. Learn to immediately turn rejection into a great motivator to propel you to find what's right for you, and to fight for it.

Within six to twelve months, I'd left Granada and landed a job in London on a new Channel 4 show as a producer director. My first big job was producing directly on the history of Africa – which took me to 22 African countries in 18 months. Everything happened to me on that job – including getting arrested – but it was all great life material. By the mid-1980s, my career was up and running as a freelance director in London making documentaries, which is what I did for the next 10 years.

← Dame Helen Mirren in her Oscar-winning performance as Queen Elizabeth II in *The Queen*, 2006

The first big break

In the mid-1980s, I met an aspiring television presenter called Jonathan Ross. His mate told me, "Jonathan wants to be David Letterman in the UK!" Jonathan had persuaded Channel 4 to give him £3,000 to explore becoming a chat show host. He and his friend begged me to ask Channel 4 for some more money. I was quite experienced by then, so Channel 4 said to me, "Oh, sure – if *you're* doing it, we'll give you £10,000." And we made this little pilot – which became *The Jonathan Ross Show*. We went round the world for several years, making crazy documentaries and having a lot of fun.

TAKEAWAY

Collaboration is crucial in building any business. This is especially true in the creative sector, where the give and take of ideas and sharing underlying trust around vision are key to the development of new creative ideas and directions. Having a good judge of character and talent is one of the most important skills you can develop in order to maximise the success of your collaborations.

Now, the thing about "talent" is that it needs looking after.

> Talent needs a partner – and a good producer is a creative partner.

I was starting to recognise that a big strength of mine was to listen to what people wanted to do and then bring the best out of them. In my mid-thirties, the penny dropped; I realised I was a facilitator and an inspirer – but chiefly, a producer.

Finding what was funny

In the early 1990s, I was invited back to Granada as Head of Comedy – a fascinating proposition, because the company didn't have any comedy at the time. I went around Manchester's comedy clubs, meeting people and laughing a lot. Performers like Steve Coogan, Caroline Aherne and John Thompson were virtually unknown – but they just oozed talent. The first time I met Steve Coogan, he invited me to see him perform at a pub. I met him for a pre-show drink, then he went off to warm up. Ten minutes later, a drunk guy at the bar tripped over and spilled beer down my front. The more he apologised, the more he kept spilling his pint on me. Foolishly, I didn't recognise this was Steve Coogan's alter ego, Paul Calf – so I felt very foolish but also very excited!

One night, we were doing a recording of stand-ups and a young Lee Evans came on and I thought, *Oh, my God, this guy's phenomenal.* He seemed very humble and unaware of just how talented he was. I signed him up, and we shot a little film – which led to his being cast in a big 20th Century Fox movie in America. So, I was just going around, finding what was funny. I developed a number of shows, working with Lee Evans, Steve Coogan, setting up the Caroline Aherne show and *The Mrs Merton Show*, which led to *The Royle Family*. *Cold Feet* was another big hit. That's when I really started to hone my talent and develop relationships.

Professional badgering

While running comedy at Granada, I interviewed to be Head of Drama. They asked, "What would you do if you took on the role?" I said I'd bring back *Prime Suspect*. It'd been off the air for about 10 years. They were surprised, but I told them, "Helen Mirren is brilliant. I don't know why you don't keep making it." So, I got the job – but then I had the terrible job of getting Helen Mirren back!

↓ Ben Miles (Detective Chief Inspector Simon Finch) and Dame Helen Mirren (Detective Superintendent Jane Tennison) in police drama *Prime Suspect: The Last Witness*, 2003

I phoned Helen's agent, who basically said, "Oh, don't be silly, she's in America now, she's not interested." I asked, "Well, can we have a cup of tea?" Anyway, badger, badger, badger – many phone calls later – she finally came into London and we had a cup of tea and she was charming and very patiently explained that she wasn't interested in reprising the role unless it was about

something meaningful. I'd already decided that's what I wanted to do. I had a story in mind for a kind of political thriller, seen through the lens of a cop. She came back to do it. And *Prime Suspect 6* won the Emmys! This put me right at the front of drama – particularly in America – so it was a real game changer.

This illustrates both the mindset of not giving up and the subtle judgement of how to badger someone professionally. If you know your idea is a winner, don't be afraid to turn your creative focus to how you can persuade a treasured collaborator that your vision fits with theirs and how you can see yourselves working together to achieve your joint goal.

A majestic epiphany

Following my epiphany that Helen Mirren should play the lead in *The Queen*, I put everything I could into getting that movie made, with Peter Morgan writing and Stephen Frears directing. When it won the Oscar, that changed everything.

At that time, I was still working for ITV as a television executive – yet I'd just produced a major hit movie. That was the watershed moment when I decided to set up my own company – mainly to have more control over the projects. It was great timing because independent companies in the UK had won the right to retain their own IP. This meant that when you sold a show to the BBC or Channel 4, you retained the intellectual property and owned the shows. This was an incredible position to be in, and one that is virtually impossible now because of streaming. There was a window of perhaps no more than 10 years, and I caught the last part of it when I set up my business.

Left Bank

Setting up Left Bank Pictures was an agonising decision. I told my wife, "It's going to take two or three years, and I can't guarantee there'll be any money."

 We set it up in 2007, and people said, "Are you mad? You're setting up a drama company in the middle of a financial crash and drama isn't really that important."

↖ Andy Harries on location with
   Matt Smith (the young Prince
   Philip) while filming *The Crown*

↑ Andy Harries with Matt Smith (the
   young Prince Philip) and Claire
   Foy (the young Queen Elizabeth)
   on the set of *The Crown*

← Andy Harries celebrating a wrap
   with Claire Foy (the young Queen
   Elizabeth) and Vanessa Kirby
   (the young Princess Margaret)
   on the set of *The Crown*

But we were all determined and disciplined and, within five years, the company was worth a hell of a lot of money – but some of that was luck.

| TAKEAWAY | Going out on your own is a massive decision. It's crucial to make sure you're at the stage of development of your business where it makes sense, given the future growth you can reasonably predict. In addition, it is key to ensure your personal finances are in shape to support your commitments – both those that are known and those that may reasonably arise. |

The title "Left Bank" came to me in the shower. The Left Bank of the Seine in Paris is traditionally associated with intellectuals of leftism and there's something quite boho about the region. I also liked "Left" because of my political inclinations – and "Bank" because it's safe.

Soon after setting up the company, I knew I wanted to plant my foot firmly in America (where I'd been building up my contacts). When I first started going to LA, no one knew who the hell I was and I'd often be siphoned off to the assistants – or even the assistants' assistants. Sometimes we just had meetings in car parks! But of course, those people moved up. Year by year, the underlings I'd met in car parks moved up the ladder and eventually became commissioners. Nurturing relationships really is key to building your reputation.

| TAKEAWAY | This is a helpful reminder that networks are everything. The relationships you make over the course of your career are not only fulfilling, but also helpful as you and your colleagues progress through the ranks. You'll find great camaraderie and support through nurturing these relationships. |

The crowning glory

The Crown was born from an idea of Peter Morgan's. He and I are deep friends and our working relationship goes back decades. He sent me a page on his initial idea about the young Elizabeth and the old Churchill. I felt it wasn't quite strong or big enough but he said, "There's more – it could be a miniseries." A week later he said, "Actually it's three series – we'll do young queen, middle-aged queen, great old queen." Two days after that he said, "It's not three – it's six." And I was like, "Jesus Christ, okay!"

He wrote a very good script about the Queen with Philip overseas. I mean, it's a great story, isn't it? Dad has smoked too many ciggies and he's on his way out. Elizabeth's newly married and she's honeymooning – then suddenly, she's 25 years old and she's the Queen. I mean, that's a fantastic start to any series.

We found ourselves in America pitching to the key broadcasters: HBO, Fox, Showtime – then Netflix on the final day. It just happened we went into Netflix at exactly the right time. They'd only just started and people didn't really know what Netflix was. But they were incredibly enthusiastic and basically said, "Yeah, it's great, we want to do it and we've got plenty of money. Let's go."

The BBC and ITV had wanted to do it, but they only had normal amounts of money. We weren't interested in normal amounts of money. We didn't want to film in 10 days – we wanted to film in 20 days, to let it breathe. We wanted the best cameraman, the best director of photography, the biggest cast. We wanted what *Harry Potter* had: the best of British acting, all wanting to appear in the show. And we pulled it off. Peter wrote pretty much 60 hours of extraordinary television (there were other contributors, but he's overseen every hour). And it took a truly great team to deliver it.

↓ Passing on lessons learned

PASSION
If you're selling, which is really the critical part of what I do, you must have so much passion, your buyer recognises and believes it. I used to say I'd lie down in front of a truck to get a commission. In 99% of your meetings, you probably won't make a sale. If you can't make a sale, make an impression. Seeds get planted and that's how creative businesses work.

FUNDING
If you've got a strong idea and you believe in yourself, you should do it. It's always good to try and get some funding if you possibly can – I think you can only go so far without a decent amount of money.

SELLING YOUR COMPANY
To play in the global market, it's definitely better to be part of a bigger, potentially global business. Most of the American studios are probably the best partners, because they've got the distribution networks, the experience and the financial security that puts people at ease.

Mindset

What is mindset?

Mindset is how you view the world, how you approach opportunities and risks and what you tell yourself about your abilities and your worth.

Growth mindset

To flourish in the business world, it's important to have a growth mindset. Entrepreneurial creatives tend to be naturally inclined to a growth mindset. They're great at problem-solving, spotting solutions others wouldn't think of.

How to cultivate a growth mindset

- **Think of problems as a positive** and see them as a challenge and opportunity for growth. If something doesn't work out, ask yourself what went right as well as what went wrong. Ask, "How will this affect my career in a positive way?" Remember, very few things go right the first time
- **Own your mistakes** as opposed to covering your tracks or blaming someone else. This inspires your team to do the same, so you can develop a culture where people aren't afraid to take risks. Mistakes are a positive. They show that you have tried and they can offer rich learnings
- **Be inspired by others** rather than envious. Instead of coveting someone else's life or career, be heartened and encouraged by what is possible – and let their accomplishments galvanise you to succeed

Why a growth mindset is crucial
- It makes you more likely to seek opportunities where others aren't looking
- It enables you to come up with solutions even in times of uncertainty

Creatives often come into their own in times of challenge. Limitations can bring out your greatest talents. If you can cultivate a growth mindset in the midst of a crisis and see openings other people miss, you have a much greater chance of success than those with a fixed mindset.

Visualisation

What is visualisation?
- Tapping into your imagination
- Thinking of something you want to achieve
- Imagining the desired outcome
- Imaging in the greatest detail possible what things look, feel, sound, and even smell like

Why visualisation is key
Research shows you have a greater chance of meeting your end goal if you imagine it has already happened. This way, when your big dream becomes a big reality, you're ready for it.

Visualisation "tricks your brain"
If you tell yourself you've done something, you start to believe you have. Your brain doesn't know the difference between real and imagined experiences. For example, if you vividly imagine climbing Mount Everest, your body buys into it and new neural pathways light up in your brain, corresponding to that "experience".

Vulnerability

How vulnerability leads to success
Vulnerability is crucial to success. We are not infallible and we can't do everything ourselves. Sometimes we need to make ourselves vulnerable and ask others for help or insights. Sometimes we need to dig deep and question ourselves.

This takes courage, which is why the act of making ourselves vulnerable is a sign of strength.

Vulnerability allows you to have perspective
It's important to know when to stop and reflect on what's working and what's not. Acknowledging a need for a change of direction can be crucial to your success.

You need to make yourself vulnerable to:
- Question whether you want to keep doing what you're doing
- Ask yourself if you need to pivot
- Look for new opportunities

Vulnerability in your team

When you're feeling pressure and struggling to manage things alone, that's the moment to reach out to your team members for help. In admitting vulnerability to your team, you will inspire them to do the same, which will promote a growth culture and mindset in turn.

Freedom to be vulnerable will give your team the confidence to:
*   Share their ideas
*   Give feedback
*   Be honest about what's really going on

Vulnerability in networking

When you feel insecure, you may try to "big yourself up" and portray confidence. But this won't bring you the desired results. Admitting the limits of your knowledge and asking the right questions is an opportunity to forge new connections.

Being vulnerable:
*   Connects you with others and helps to spark other opportunities
*   Enables you to reach out and ask for what you need with authenticity
*   Can be disarming and attractive, creating an instant rapport

A key reminder...
*   Don't make yourself vulnerable to everyone all the time
*   Use your instinct to choose the right moment and the right people

Developing grit and resilience

Grit is the determination and stamina to keep going until you get there. When you really love something, this naturally gives you a lot of grit. But grit alone won't get you there – you also need resilience.

Resilience is the ability to bounce back – for example from feedback or rejection. If you can't bounce back from setbacks (resilience) you'll find it really hard to keep going (grit).

The best way to build grit is to build resilience, because it is linked to:

- Self-belief
- Confidence
- Vulnerability
- Overcoming imposter syndrome
- Preventing procrastination

Two ways to build your resilience

1. Adopt a growth mindset

Rejection or negative feedback is nearly always painful in the moment. But it's important to adopt a growth mindset, as discussed above. Reflect on the experience, find the positives, ask, "What can I learn from this?" Then make the improvements and move forward.

2. Give yourself creative breaks

It's important to schedule in time for creative breaks. They are serious business – put them in your calendar, or they'll never happen. They should be fun and playful, and completely different from what you're used to – for example, a life-drawing class, a fascinating exhibition, or a lesson in a craft or sport you've never tried before. Don't mistake creative breaks for something frivolous. Science shows they make you less likely to become stressed, burnt out and overwhelmed.

Zone of genius

Working in your zone of genius

You're in your zone of genius when you're doing that one thing only *you* can do. You love it and it comes so naturally. It's where you should be spending most of your time.

If you find yourself spending many hours outside your zone of genius – i.e. continuously struggling to do something you're not naturally good at – it's important to recognise the cost that has to your overall mindset.

PRIYA AHLUWALIA

The Sustainable Fashion Trailblazer

Priya Ahluwalia

Founder of fashion label Ahluwalia

It's another day of lockdown in London and Priya Ahluwalia receives an unexpected email. She's only two years out of university where her graduate show was a smash hit, drawing orders from Opening Ceremony in New York and LN-CC in London, the widely acknowledged arbiters of new fashion cool. That was before she even had a logo. And then the pandemic hit.

The email she receives is from Gucci. She only finds it while clearing her spam folder, and thinks it's clearly just an advert. As she starts to hit delete, something makes her open it. Much to her surprise, it is a direct message from Gucci – the actual Gucci – addressed to her personally. As there are no physical runway shows, the email reads, they are starting an online event called "GucciFest", a ten-part short film drama series, like a TV series, in which young designers would tell stories using their designs. They had been researching young designers who they wanted to support via the series. Not only do they want to commission Priya, they want her to open the festival.

From boring lockdown spam to jubilation in 30 seconds flat. Priya created a film called *Joy*. She knew what she wanted to do and what the film would be, but she didn't know how to execute a film, so she worked with a great co-director Samona Olanipekin, himself a new director, who was mentored by artist and filmmaker Steve McQueen (Oscar-winning director of *12 Years a Slave,* etc). *Joy* is a celebration of the Black British experience, expressed through a series of stories with a cast of people who were either involved in the Black Civil Rights Movement in the UK, athletes who symbolise strength or chosen to show family unity and love – all expressions of joy.

"I remember standing on set one day and thinking, *This is one of the best days of my life,*" Priya says. "I still feel that to this day – I get really emotional talking about it. The film was incredibly well-received and it was life-changing for me. First, the opportunity to do GucciFest, and second, what that film has done for the rest of my life – without it, we wouldn't be sitting in this Studio in Soho.

↗ Ahluwalia AW23 Collection "Symphony" in St John's Smith Square, a London church converted to a concert hall, set to music Priya called "the soundtrack to my life"

↓ Priya Ahluwalia: Highlights

- Born and raised in London to and Indian mother and Nigerian father
- Masters in Menswear from Westminster University
- H&M Design Award
- LVMH Prize
- British Fashion Awards "Leader of Change" three years in a row
- Queen Elizabeth II Award for British Design 2021
- British *GQ* Menswear Fund

- *Vogue* Forces for Change Award
- Collaborations including Adidas, Ganni, Mulberry, Paul Smith, Gucci
- Invented the Circulate digital platform for Microsoft, whereby consumers can upcycle their old clothes for use in Ahluwalia fashion collections
- Signed as a film director to Ridley Scott's Black Dog Films
- Cover of British *Vogue* January 2024 as a fashion sustainability trailblazer

↑→ Stills from Priya's short
film *Beloved*, her first
with Ridley Scott's Black
Dog Films

"It was also such a pivotal moment in my life because, not only did I fall in love with film, I also realised film could help me expand both my creativity and my business. I saw that I needed to diversify my business: a fashion wholesale is not the easiest way to make money, especially as it's so affected by the temperamental economy. And I also love the fact that working on a film is so creative, which helps my fashion work. Also, being digital, film is so democratic – it tells stories immediately and everywhere, available to everyone forever. I love both fashion and film, I couldn't give one up. I just have to work all the hours under the sun.

"The GucciFest commission was a life-changing moment and I leaned into it, and worked hard to see what other opportunities it could create."

Priya is a pioneer of her generation in both sustainable fashion and story-led filmmaking. Her unique, London-based fashion brand Ahluwalia tells the stories of her dual Indian and Nigerian family heritage using only vintage and deadstock materials. Since her sold-out MA graduate show at Westminster University, Ahluwalia has taken the fashion and environmental worlds by storm.

I spoke with Priya in her Ahluwalia studio in London's Soho.

The beginnings

I was born and raised in London. I've known I wanted to be a fashion designer since I was about five years old. So, I tailored my education towards fashion. I was always academic at school and my family are Indian and Nigerian, so they were all quite apprehensive about my pursuing fashion. They wanted me to be successful and happy and thought that fashion was a really hard business to break through in. I don't blame people for being scared of it as a career choice. I do think it is really difficult for people who are really into the design but don't want to think about business or marketing – to be independent and commercially successful, you need to be thinking about both.

I did a BA and then an MA in menswear at Westminster University. I always knew I wanted to design for all people, but you had to select either men's or women's, so I chose men's, as I'd been doing that for quite a while. And there were so many women's brands, I thought if I did something in the menswear space, people were more likely to notice. On my MA I was encouraged to figure out my own path and what my unique view is, which was crucial for developing my brand.

A family journey of awakening

During my MA, I visited my Dad in Nigeria. At one point I was in a huge traffic jam and noticed all the hawkers selling things to people who were stuck in their cars. I realised they were all wearing second-hand clothing, but it was all European. For example, T-shirts for the London 2012 Olympics and I even saw one from the Leicester Fun Run, which was crazy. I was really curious about that, so I did some research and learned a lot about the second-hand clothing trade and how 80 per cent of the clothes we give to charity in Britain are sent to the global south for recycling or dumping.

Researching further into the life of a second hand garment, I learned about the city of Panipat, 90 miles north of Delhi in India, which is the biggest centre for garment recycling in the world – and the other half of my heritage. I went to stay with some cousins who live near there. I took my camera and photographed it. The clothes, scraps and threads are all sorted by colour into piles. So you go into these huge warehouses and it could be a massive orange room, or piles of red or pink or blue. Knowing what it is, it's shocking, but it's also visually striking and beautiful.

The birth of a brand vision

I learned a lot there and it changed the ethos of how I wanted to design.

I always knew I wanted to explore and celebrate my heritage because, at least not until recently, I don't think Black and brown ideas have been celebrated very much in European fashion in a way that's not cultural appropriation. But seeing first-hand the environmental and cultural impact of this massive second-hand garment infrastructure made me see an intersection between a brand that celebrates my heritage creatively but also one that, in the way it executes, makes products and experiences that are better for people and the planet.

When I was leaving university, on the day of my graduate show I also released my book, actually a little zine, called *Sweet Lassi* which featured the photos I'd taken on my two revelatory trips and told the story of what I had discovered. *i-D* and *Dazed* wrote about it. That catapulted my brand to a whole new level. All of a sudden, two stores approached me – Opening Ceremony and LN-CC – asking to make an order for my final collection. And I thought, *Well, OK, I'm starting this business now.*

↑ Images from Priya's first book *Sweet Lassi*, inspired by her revelatory family trips to Lagos, Nigeria and Panipat, India in 2017. The second-hand clothes and excess piles of textiles she saw led to her focus on sustainable fashion.

I now realise I was naturally good at marketing and getting a message out, taking an opportunity and magnifying it by making a buzz and co-opting it for something else. My graduate show was the most spoken about in my year. I think that was not only because of the clothes, but because of my messages – and I think the timing of it was really good.

| TAKEAWAY | **You may not have thought of the label "good at marketing" as applying to yourself, just as Priya hadn't originally. As with her own example, marketing is really about understanding which authentic messages about your brand are the most inspiring and exciting, and then spotting opportunities to get those messages out there. Priya created a zine telling the story of her brand journey and released it on the same day as her graduate show. You don't have to be uber confident or enjoy being the centre of attention to be good at creating buzz. You just need to be an empathetic observer of which authentic messages stand out and spot opportunities to amplify them.** |

Building a business

My mum is a financial director, so she was a great help in figuring out the fundamentals like securing trademarks, the company structure and other key details. We set it all up very quickly. I knew I wanted to do a new collection, but had no idea how I was going to present it or where. The British Fashion Council had picked up on what I was doing, but the brand was too young for their New Gen programme, which funds and mentors emerging designers. But they gave me an area to display my new collection during London Fashion Week.

That turned out to be huge, because Adidas saw that display and asked me to do a fully fledged runway show as part of the upcoming Paris Fashion Week. That was my first runway show and it was incredible. David Beckham and Pharrell were there. That took the brand to a different stratosphere.

Growing a business is so much about understanding an opportunity and then seeing how you can create the next opportunity out of that. And a lot of it is because I think I'm a people person – at the end of the day it's only human beings who do business. So being able to get on with people and show how you bring them value or show why your ideas will make their ideas even better – those things are really important.

I want to have a brand that grows into a lifestyle brand so we can do lots of different things. It's about people, getting your ideas out into the world and making money from it.

 Whether you want to have billions in the bank or just enough money to make your next project, it's business that lets you do that.

"Connection" vs the dreaded "Networking"

Building good relationships is key. I hate the word "networking" – it doesn't have to mean some sort of seminar where you wear a name tag. But going out to certain places where you bump into people, you meet people, and mingling with people who are also trying to work on the same dream, no matter what stage of their career they're at, is really beneficial. "Networking" has such a corny corporate vibe to it. But it's really just connecting with people. No person is an island, no person can create and build these amazing businesses on their own. If you look at any successful business person, there's always a team that helped them get there. So, it's important to find your people – people who believe in you but who can also challenge you, and people you also believe in. I ran into a friend at the library today who's a costume designer. We started talking and the back and forth spurred a whole bunch of new ideas for each of us. That's why "networking" is great. It's not only about

← Priya with David Beckham, Pharrell Williams, Paolina Russo and Nicholas Daley at the Adidas AW 2019 show in Paris

↑ Priya using her
revolutionary app,
Circulate, designed
to reduce fabric waste
by allowing people to
upcycle their garments

→ Circulate features open
calls for clothing needed
for upcoming Ahluwalia
collections – if you have
the appropriate piece, it
can be sent in and upcycled
in the Ahluwalia studio

practical things, like "I'm looking for a photographer", it's about meeting people with whom you can discuss and grow your ideas. It's a key part of the creative process, that back and forth.

One of the most crucial pieces of advice about building your own business is to recognise how crucial informal networks are. While the formal networks of conferences, seminars and the like are crucial as well, it's easy to overlook how the informal gatherings of like-minded people – which may seem just social or to be focused solely on your creative (vs business) interests – are crucial as well. It's the spontaneous conversations which can often spark the biggest lightbulb moments and also lead to opportunities or new contacts you hadn't known of before.

Growing the business

After the Adidas Paris show in January 2019, we started picking up more stores and sales were increasing. I've been honoured the brand has received many awards, and each time we do, it really does open new opportunities – people want to buy more or partner with you more, and you also meet more people. I introduced womenswear and that really changed things. Having started out in menswear, I always knew I wanted to do womenswear, but introducing it takes a lot of time. I didn't have the capacity at the beginning, but people kept asking me when I was going to introduce it. When I had my first employee, we started womenswear, and it was great. It was successful straightaway and has become really popular now.

And then there was Covid, which was a really scary time. But it also made me think about diversifying. I ended up doing a lot of brand partnerships, both individually as well as my brand. I did a collaboration with Ganni for a few years, which was actually how I launched womenswear, and also collaborations with Paul Smith for menswear and Mulberry for bags.

Harnessing tech to pioneer new spaces

In 2021 I did a tech-focused collaboration with Microsoft. They said, "Why don't you think about a problem you're having in your business and how tech could be the solution?" So I designed a platform called Circulate that uses AI to crowdsource people's unwanted clothing. Ahluwalia puts out a call out for a certain type of garment, for example, denim. Users take a photo of their unwanted garment and upload it to the Circulate platform, then we use AI to categorise it and make sure it's in acceptable condition.

If we accept it, we send the user a prepaid postage label, they send it to us and we use the fabric in our collections. In return they get discount points against products on our website. It allows people to engage with sustainability and with our brand, while also building our community and retaining customers, so it's been really interesting.

We also partnered with Microsoft to create QR codes to accompany Ahluwalia clothing, so customers can scan them to find out information about their garments and their origins and the story behind the Ahluwalia brand. Growing a business is so much about understanding an opportunity and then seeing how you can create the next opportunity out of it.

Film as an expansion of the brand and storytelling

After *Joy*, the film I made for GucciFest, I was working on a partnership with Dropbox and they wanted to do some sort of event. I said, "Why don't we do a film and I can direct it?" Which I did. After that, every time I could get funding, I would make a film because I loved it. I loved the storytelling and that I was learning so much about cameras and editing, it was like going back to school in a way.

About a year and a half ago I was approached by Ridley Scott's Black Dog Film agency – on LinkedIn actually – so random! They're an agency for directors but also a production company. They said they wanted to talk about my films, so I thought I was walking into a sales meeting where they were going to pitch me to produce the films that I work on for brands like Mulberry.

But instead they said, "We see something interesting in your work and we want you to consider signing with us as a film director." I couldn't process it at first. I think especially as a woman, it can feel scary to be a polymath and to step outside of our normal area, like people are going to judge us for it. But I realised then, if I don't know something, I'm just going to learn it. That's the thing about being an entrepreneur or a creative; you learn something new every day. I had a really good feeling about the team there, and it turns out I was right.

Since then, Black Dog has produced a short film that I created about Nollywood and Bollywood cinema called *Beloved*. At the time, my Autumn/Winter 2022 collection was about to come out in the shops, so we created an Ahluwalia Film Festival at Soho House to celebrate the film's release. We screened it and we had an

↑ Still from Priya's first short film, *Joy*, commissioned by Gucci and made in collaboration with director Samona Olanipekin

Ahluwalia pop-up shop and a party – that's how we also announced my signing with Black Dog. Since then, I've directed a music video, plus films for Nike, Levi's and the Design Museum. Now our studio is based in the Ridley Scott building, a really smart building in Soho, and that all started because of the Gucci commission.

Film has become a big part of what I do and crucial to growing my business.

Surviving the side-effects of business growth

For Ahluwalia the rough patches didn't come at the very beginning but a few years in. In the beginning, while I was hustling and doing all the designs myself, I didn't have expectations and I didn't have major responsibilities. If it didn't work, it would be fine because I could just do something else.

What changes when your business gets bigger is that you have responsibility for more things. You have employees, your premises, your stores and customers – there are a lot more things. In my opinion, that feels like more pressure than the beginning. You also have less time to do the things you really love and make you stay creative.

We're only human beings and we can't be perfect all the time. Hard and heartbreaking things can come up in your personal life, and you still have to turn up to work and be everyone's boss. As a team, we're quite open about things going on in our lives so we can be aware if there are people not able to turn up for work as their best selves and we can compensate for it to make sure the job gets done.

| TAKEAWAY | **Building a group of loyal and supportive people around you is absolutely key. As an entrepreneur, this means both your internal team, external advisors and collaborators and your wider network of friends, family and mentors. You will learn from them, as they'll learn from you, and when times get tough, their support will be crucial, and you'll be able to do the same for them. It's a truly virtuous circle and also great for your happiness and wellbeing.** |

Building strong foundations

Life is full of curveballs. Some of them are fantastic and some of them are horrible and hideous. I think if you want to be a creative and an entrepreneur, it's so important to have your people, to know who they are. When a close family relative of mine suddenly passed away recently, a close friend and also a colleague who did sales drove to my house, which was also where my studio was. I couldn't do anything. He packed all the orders for the stores and got me through. People help lift you up. When I've had friends having a hard time, I do the same for them. It's not for the faint-hearted, having your own business. That's why it's really important to make sure you have a good support network.

It's also crucial that you've laid down a strong foundation for your business, including key systems and processes, so that others can come in and help you keep things going based on the template for your business you've created. You've got to be prepared to roll with the punches.

↓ Passing on lessons learned

TEAM MEMBERS ARE CRUCIAL
I work so closely with people who are not on our internal team – for example, with our Ahluwalia stylist and casting director. They're such a crucial part of the brand, they've helped literally to define an "Ahluwalia person". And I couldn't have made the brand without my hugely talented internal team. No person is an island, and it's also so important to give your team credit whenever you can.

WALK BEFORE YOU CAN RUN
I'd love to expand into new areas right now, like homeware. But I know I don't have the bandwidth at the moment. So I'll be disciplined about keeping my focus on Ahluwalia's menswear, womenswear and our new footwear – and keep evaluating when it makes sense to expand to other areas.

INTERROGATE YOUR VISION
Really understand and hone what your point of view on anything is. What is your creative point of view and what sets your idea apart from anyone else's? Do you like the colour red? If not, why? Really think about it deeply.

LEARN EVERY PART OF YOUR BUSINESS AS WELL AS YOUR CRAFT
Another piece of advice, more practically, is to understand and learn every part of your business. For example, if you want to be a fashion designer, figure out production, figure out social media, figure out fabric sourcing. Learn every single element that you can in your practice so that when you're running a team, you know how to guide them but you also know what they shouldn't be doing. Make sure you're aware of the specific skill sets that it takes to run your business. If you don't know about a specific area already, do some work experience, take a course or find a mentor to learn from.

When you start, the buck stops with you: you've got to do everything. At the beginning, I was designing, pattern cutting, sewing, packing, shipping. That's fine, I can sew, I can make a pair of jeans. But at some point you need others to take over those areas – the key is to know the craft yourself.

BE RELENTLESS ABOUT TRACKING SPENDING
On the purely business side, at the beginning, check all of your spending. What are you spending and why? That three metres of fabric, what is it for? The development of a custom thing, or is it for an actual season? Track all of the money because when things start growing more quickly you'll need to make your budgets. And without the knowledge of what you spent before, it's really hard to move forward.

Mentors

Having a great mentor can be life changing. Especially in the early days, being able to pick the brains of someone who is further along in their journey, has experience and perspective you don't have and who supports your goals, is transformative.

What does a mentor do?

Being an entrepreneur is tough, and you can't go it alone. A mentor is an experienced individual who can help you develop your business goals and provide valuable insight into any challenges you may face or tricky decisions you have to make.

Your mentor might come from your creative sector or from a different world altogether. The key here is that you get on well, hold a mutual respect and can discuss issues openly.

If you connect with the right person as your mentor, it can develop into a long-lasting partnership benefitting both you and your business. Starting out on your own can be lonely, so having someone to talk things through with and bounce ideas off in a non-judgemental way can be invaluable.

Why mentors can play an important role

There is no set or defined role for a mentor. This relationship will evolve alongside you and your business. But a mentor can be crucial in helping you see the bigger picture. They might inspire you to be even more creative, connect you with valuable contacts or communities, coax you out of your comfort zone and encourage you to look around corners and consider different possibilities. Importantly, a mentor offers a safe space in which to learn and experiment.

Mentorship is a way of absorbing knowledge and experience from those who've been there and done that. It's a priceless opportunity to ask all those difficult questions that need answering when you don't know where to turn for advice. Finally, a mentor can also act as a backstop check. When you're making important decisions, it's worthwhile having someone you trust to sense-check your instincts.

Mentors vs. coaches

Mentors offer their time for free, whereas coaches are paid-for external collaborators. However, mentoring is still a professional activity, not a charitable one. It's a meaningful commitment for you both.

How to find the right mentor

A mentor can be anyone. They don't have to be older or at a certain stage in their career; they could also be a peer offering advice and guidance from a different angle or area of expertise. Mentors generally want to pay it forward – perhaps they had a great mentor to guide them in the past. Entrepreneurs can also have more than one mentor. We all have varying skills and experiences, so sometimes it's helpful to build a relationship with a couple of mentors who help you with different sides of the business.

Find a mentor you identify with, who you feel comfortable with. This means pairing up with someone who has similar guiding values and a similar approach to business. It's a person you click with, first and foremost.

You might find that tracking their career or achievements has been enlightening for you and resonates with your own journey. You might want to emulate what they've done, or you might respect their approach to business and people. If you feel like you're watching a more experienced version of yourself in action, it's a good sign that they are the right fit.

Sometimes, entrepreneurs choose a mentor with a style diametrically opposed to their own. This kind of relationship can present huge growth opportunities. Their approach might scare you, but learning to adopt skills outside your own toolkit enables you to grow as a business leader, and as a person. This approach isn't for everyone, but it's not to be discounted.

Finding the right mentor can be game-changing

Thomas Heatherwick

How to make a mentor relationship work

- **Know what you want to get out of the partnership** – be up front from the beginning about why you need a mentor, as this should influence your choice. Does the mentor have time to dedicate to your business? They might not be in the same field as you, but be clear about the skills and advice you're looking for
- **Be flexible** – while it's vital to have goals as a mentee, do stay open to other possibilities
- **Communicate openly and always ask questions** – don't turn up to mentor meetings thinking they will lead the conversation. Control the talking points, come prepared, and always ask searching, challenging questions
- **Value your mentor's time** – as a successful person, your mentor is likely to have a busy schedule. Don't waste your conversations together, particularly as mentors often give their time pro bono
- **Respect your mentor's privacy** – settle on your communication channels and stick to this agreement. No one likes to be bombarded with messages or contacted out of hours if that's not what's been agreed
- **Put your learnings into action** – the best gift you can give someone who is dedicating their precious time to your development is to act on the advice they've offered. This doesn't mean you always have to do exactly as they advise, but your success will reflect well on them in turn
- **Show appreciation** – as mentors are generally unpaid, you can deepen your partnership by offering gratitude for their support: never forget to say thank you

> Take advice. When you're starting something, it's a difficult balancing act between staying true to your vision and taking advice when people tell you that's a really bad idea and you're going to have to change it. That is the trick.

Matthew Slotover

C ,

A mentor is someone who allows
you to see the hope inside yourself.

Oprah Winfrey

THOMAS HEATHERWICK

The Design Revolutionary

Thomas Heatherwick
Founder of Heatherwick Studio

When fashion designer Diane von Furstenberg and her husband Barry Diller, media powerhouse and former head of Hollywood studios Paramount and Fox, visited the Shanghai World Expo in 2010, they happened upon the British Pavilion. What they saw took their breath away: a giant rounded cube with 66,000 clear fibre-optic rods sticking out in all directions, swaying in the breeze, the tip of each containing seeds from an endangered plant species. It was called The Seed Cathedral.

Designed by the enterprising British designer Thomas Heatherwick, it took conceptual cues from a world-leading plant preservation project at London's Kew Gardens and visual cues from, well… a 1970s advert for the Play-Doh Mop Top Hair Shop toy. Thomas called it a "hairy building". Barry Diller called it "one of the most dazzling things I've ever seen." It won the Expo's top design prize. Equally impressive, given that it cost half of what the other countries' pavilions cost.

A few years later, following Thomas's breakout "Cauldron" for the 2012 London Olympics, Diller and von Furstenberg were looking for someone to help them create a new landmark for New York City. The site was the crumbling Pier 54, just off Manhattan's West Side Highway, where survivors of the *Titanic* had been brought after rescue in 1912, and from where the ill-fated *Lusitania* had set sail in 1915. Along with the other piers lining the Hudson River, it had declined along with ocean liner travel. Whoever took on the brief needed to understand the history of the site and also have the imagination to realise a groundbreaking public space that rose above the mighty Hudson River.

Von Furstenburg and Diller called Thomas, and Little Island was born in 2021. With a clear structural link to the Seed Cathedral, it's an undulating parallelogram supported by 132 tulip-shaped concrete pylons that are "planters" for hundreds of plant species, with an amphitheatre at its centre. Like the Seed Cathedral and the Olympic Cauldron, it comprises separate multiples brought together into a cohesive whole, symbolising the building of community – in this case in a derelict part of Manhattan.

↗ "Seed Cathedral", the UK Pavilion
for the Shanghai World Expo in 2010
designed by Heatherwick Studio

↓ Thomas Heatherwick: Highlights

- Born and raised in London
- Studied 3-D Design at Manchester Polytechnic and design at the Royal College of Art
- Launched Heatherwick Studio in 1994
- Not trained as an architect; his practice spans product design and interiors, architecture and urban planning
- Creative highlights include: Harvey Nichols windows for London Fashion Week 1997, The Rolling Bridge 2004, The UK Pavilion for the Shanghai World Expo 2010, New London Routemaster Bus 2010, The Olympic Cauldron for the 2012 London Olympics, Little Island, New York City, Tree of Trees Sculpture for the Queen's Jubilee 2022

- Awards include: Prince Phillip Designers Prize 2006, The London Design Medal 2010, Tokyo Design and Art Environmental Award for designer of the year, 2010, RIBA Lubetkin Prize, 2010, Compasso d'Oro, 2014, CBE for services to the design industry
- Published his book, *Humanise* in 2023 and its accompanying campaign against boring buildings

Like most of Thomas's projects, it sparked wonder and delight, as well as a good dose of criticism from the sharp-elbowed world of architecture because of its fearless originality. It's this originality that has defined Thomas at every turn. His steadfast commitment to ideas that reject dogma and conventional wisdom mean his unbridled imagination can be put to work in the service of wonder, playfulness and humanity. It also meant he could build Heatherwick Studio, a thriving creative business that now employs over 200 people who continue to delight in this way of seeing and making the world.

I spoke with Thomas at Heatherwick Studio in King's Cross, London.

The seeds of creativity

I feel like I'm quite a logical outcome of the people around me. My grandmother was a German Jewish avant-garde designer, who studied at the Berlin equivalent of the Bauhaus. In 1939, in her early 20s, she had two minutes to escape the SS, or she would have been taken to a concentration camp. She narrowly escaped and came to the UK on her own. She then got people to help her to get her family – her parents, and brother and sister – out of Germany to escape persecution.

She was a dynamic, determined, hardworking, artistically uncompromising woman. After escaping to London, she was immersed in the arts: first she worked for the London-based Hungarian modernist architect Erno Goldfinger (designer of the north London brutalist icon, the Trellick Tower), then she was asked by Marks and Spencer to set up their first textile design studio.

She left Marks and Spencer and the design world after 10 years and pioneered art therapy (a new area at the time). She returned to Germany to work with children of the Nazi generation, helping them cope with what their parent's generation had done. Which was seen as particularly impactful, as she had been of the generation persecuted. She was an incredibly inspiring figure in my life, with her fascination with beauty, her avant-garde clothes and jewellery and her modernist apartment.

My grandfather was a writer, and very interested in innovations of the Industrial Revolution engineers. I used to enjoy looking through his books and seeing the utterly world-changing, ambitious achievements that were happening at the end of the 19th century. They gave me a sense of what was possible.

Becoming a maker

 I grew up making things, drawing, always very interested in inventions.

To my surprise, you couldn't study inventing. Invention itself, though celebrated in Edwardian and Victorian times, often had the word "mad" next to it. You're a "mad inventor", with the image of Chitty Chitty Bang Bang or something like that!

I spent my childhood having ideas and experimenting and inventing. In my home that was very easy, as there was an endless supply of tools and materials because my mum – a jeweller, enameller and painter – had a workshop, with kilns, pliers, a workbench, chemicals... you name it. I admired that she could make and fix things. I subsequently discovered that the world of designing buildings was disconnected from making; it was sort of anti-making. It was sort of anti-people really, as well – without realising it. Because it celebrated theory and the cerebral – not the heart or the hand.

← The Olympic Cauldron, made for the 2012 London Olympics, featured 204 copper pieces, one for each participating country, that burned together as a symbol of peace and unity

↗ Thomas with his mentor, Sir
Terence Conran in "Gazebo",
Thomas's student thesis
project at the RCA –
a double-helix structure
in stacked plywood

↑ Model for Thomas's first
building, based on twisting
objects, made while a student
at Manchester Polytechnic

→ The finished product:
Thomas's completed first
building, fully designed
and constructed while at
Manchester Polytechnic

Architecture vs buildings

I was lucky that I got to go to Manchester Polytechnic, where I spent three years studying 3D Design. That was where I built my first building. I was 21 and spurred on by my surprise to discover that no one there ever built buildings. Thousands of people were trained to *design* buildings, but no one ever made anything! If you think about it, buildings are the biggest objects in the world that humans can make, you really need to be a maker to understand what that means: to understand what it means to shape clay or carve wood or stone, and really feel how the light falls across things. I discovered that in architecture, "making" wasn't a thing.

My dissertation was on the education of building designers, and I discovered something bizarre: the makers of the biggest objects in the world didn't work on building sites in the holidays, had never mixed concrete, had never laid a brick, had never done joinery. It was an intellectualised profession disconnected from the real world. It was like The Emperor's New Clothes. I realised that from the practical world I'd come from, where people made things, that that was a space – and my dissertation proved that.

 So, I told my tutor I wanted to make a building, and he said, "No, make a model."

I went to the architecture department and said, "Why don't we build a real building?" And the lecturer there looked at me and said, "Show me your design." So, I showed the design. And then he said, "What's the poetry of your design?" And I said, "Poetry? Well, the design is based on twisting objects." And then he stopped, looked up, and said, "That isn't architecture." That's when I realised that they thought a building and architecture are two different things, but they're not. I realised the word "architecture" was a big compliment to be bestowed on what was deemed to be a worthy design. But the reality is that all buildings are architecture. Think about it like chair design: you can look at a chair and think, *That's bad chair design*, but you still know it's a chair.

That lecturer refused to help me. But luckily, the department of three-dimensional design – wood, metal, ceramic, glass and plastics – got behind me and helped me get 26 funding sponsors, and I built the building.

Never ignore your instincts: what they are telling you is correct, at least for you. In the face of accepted wisdom and definitions, if you don't think things look right, listen to it. That could be the core of your big insight, revealing how there is always a different way of looking at things than the way they always have been – that's where innovation comes from.

 That gave me immense confidence and lit a fire inside.

Not in an arrogant way, it just made me realise that there's a gap. That everyone from the technical side of 3-D design got behind my building, but not the building department! This was about 10 years before the Serpentine did their first Summer Pavilion celebrating architecture.

Then I went to the Royal College of Art for two years for a masters degree, which I knew was the run-up to being on your own. I wrote my thesis, a manifesto of "What should I do?" in order to help me think, *How would I do this work, filling the gap between architecture and making?* In a sense, it was my artistic business plan. And it's spooky, pulling it out again now, 29 years later, because it's exactly what I'm doing now.

Striking out on my own

By the time I finished the Royal College of Art, I'd totalled seven years of studying design and I was conscious I was going to fall off the conveyor belt of academia into the entire rest of my life. So, at the same time as studying, I spent my last year thinking about what I was going to do after – and I decided to set up my own practice.

I suppose I couldn't see anyone else to work for. Because it seemed that there was a gap in a way of thinking about bringing ideas into the world of cities and buildings. So I decided to set up my own practice.

There are many factors to consider in deciding to go out on your own, including how you will find the revenue streams to support yourself. If you're committed to doing that and have found enough sources of revenue, present and future, then go for it.

↑ "Bayview", Google's worldwide headquarters in Silicon Valley overlooking San Francisco Bay. A series of sweeping canopies with a "dragon scale" roof delivers Google's ambition for a human-centric, sustainable and innovative space.

When I started I had no projects, and it was terrifying. I'd assumed I'd be stuck in obscurity because of my interest in innovation and ideas, which I assumed society didn't want. But I was lucky; the Crafts Council gave me a grant to help set up a workspace and buy some tools to make the models of projects.

I knew I couldn't afford both a studio and a home – so it had to be the same place. I found a small building that had been a button factory in Camden Town, where I could both live and work. In the main workspace there was a water tank, so I put my bed behind it so no one could see there was a bed there. If someone was coming for a meeting I had to make sure there were no bread crumbs on the table. When I had to have a shower because I was about to have a meeting, I had to creep past one or two of my team.

In the beginning, you need lots of help – and I was lucky; a lot of people helped me. Maybe it was because I looked so needy, so people took pity on me. There was someone who had been a year below me at Manchester who helped me immensely to start the studio. We all worked for virtually nothing.

And a neighbour pulled me aside and showed me how to do that sort of multi-bar accounting in an accounting book. I got too interested in it. I'd go out, buy some screws and tools, come back, get the receipt, staple it into the accounting book, write it in, write down the VAT (sales tax), and then you'd think, *Ah, I'll have a juice to drink now* – and you'd think you'd done something – but you hadn't done anything! So I had to push that aside.

I tried to be very careful. I didn't have any business partner at the beginning because all the people I've met who had business partners always fell out with them. I just knew I didn't want that misery that I'd seen other people get stuck in. I knew I had no other plan; this was me.

Having a business partner is a very personal decision. Having one can be wonderful for dividing the workload, comparing notes, sharing complementary skill sets and weathering the ups and downs together. On the other hand, it's great to have free rein to pursue the vision for the business on your own and often visions can differ if others are involved. So, carefully think through whether a partner makes sense for you.

This was sometimes lonely; a business partner is a comrade, someone to figure things out with, and I lacked that. But that meant the people who worked with me were my comrades. In some organisations with just a couple of founders, I think the juicy conversations tend to happen between those two founders,

← Coal Drops Yard was originally two elongated elevated railway tracks with attached warehouses used to transport and store coal when it was Victorian London's fuel source. Heatherwick Studio radically reimagined the dilapidated structures to create a lively retail district.

with everyone else left out cold around the outside. I didn't have a co-founder or main partner, so there was a genuine striving all together. It's enjoyable to be part of that striving, you know, and not feel you're just hearing the news afterwards.

Building a business

I've done a couple of hundred projects over the last 29 years, but the biggest project I've ever done, by a long way – the perpetual one that has used the most of my thinking – has been the studio itself, as a project. If you have an interest in excellence in projects, you have to be interested in excellence of organisation. That means optimising people, tuning into people's passions and making a place where you can co-create.

It's funny when I hear people starting businesses saying, "I've started my business and by the end of the year it will be profitable." It took me many, many years to make a profit at all – I didn't know what a profit was. I struggled for many years. But I think the profit was projects. It was managing to do a project at all.

 It's important to not think of profit as money only; there are different ways we can see a positive outcome to what we do.

← Coal Drops Yard: the gabled roofs of the two buildings join to form a new upper story giving an unexpected new view over London.

It was a number of years until it was possible to have some money to reinvest to do things.

I believed that what I did was useful to society and could bring benefit and pleasure to many people. And bit by bit, gradually, I got those chances. It was a painful process – because I'd never worked for anyone else, I had no shorthand. I had no sense of how to run a project, how to even write the letters necessary to *getting* a project. I was almost designing a new logo every time I wrote a letter to someone, making business cards myself... there were no systems.

Being trusted is a very slow process. Big buildings cost tens of millions, even hundreds of millions (the Google projects we're designing now are valued at over $1 billion). These are pieces of a city which are major long-term commitments. But you don't get to this position quickly. I was very lucky along the way to have a few people commission me because I didn't claim to be an expert, and I learned immense amounts from them.

The art of co-creation

At the Royal College of Art, it was very hard to get in there, everyone was very high-achieving. I remember on the first day a number of them looked like it was a huge accolade they were there, that it was proof that they were a genius after all.

Studying is a funny thing, particularly in creative subjects, because the emphasis is on the individual – there's a fetishisation of genius, of individual brilliance. At the Royal College of Art, I felt I could design OK by myself, sitting scrunching up your brain trying to be brilliant, imagining your heroes who had just sat there being brilliant. But I actually realised I felt like I had a disability, because, for example, when the structural engineer came in once a week to our department, and he and I sat together, it was like the flowers bloomed and the lights went on. Together we bounced ideas around, the ideas shot in every direction. We forgot who was the designer and who was the engineer, and sometimes I would be engineering and he would be coming up with design thoughts and directions. It didn't matter: design wasn't in me or him, it was between us.

I thought there was something wrong with me, that I needed other people, until I realised that collaboration was what let me be good.

↑ Little Island: 2.4-acre artificial island adjacent to Manhattan's Meatpacking District and the High Line, with the amphitheatre at top left, and undulating trails and gardens planted with 390 species of vegetation.

→ Pre-cast concrete "planters" rise above the Hudson River at the site of previously demolished derelict Pier 54, where ocean liners docked a century ago and where the *Titanic* survivors arrived in 1912

I'm continuously growing a team of brilliant collaborators where we trust each other and can be silly together and people feel safe to try ideas out. It's a never-ending project, you're always growing and evolving, with new team members joining.

 The best thing is when, at the end of a brainstorm, you cannot say exactly where the ideas came from.

My job is to somehow sit in the middle of that conversation on every project. We're all a bit disappointed when it's me who comes up with the ideas on a project!

It's wonderful when it's the accumulation of this person's idea and that person's experience and even when you ask one of the youngest team members – who might not have had the confidence to speak up – "What do you think?" and they express what you all feel underneath and you know it's absolutely right and it changes everything. It's lovely for them to see that people who have been doing something for many more years and have more qualifications than them, that the project can change because of some insight that they had. And it's not just ideas, it's also perspective – perspective can knock everything into a different place.

TAKEAWAY

The best thing about creativity is the collaboration: working together as a team to come up with an amazing new idea and a plan for how to get it done. And the most effective thing is to involve people from all areas and from senior to junior – that's how you make sure you get the best ideas.

Breakthrough moments

The first one breakthrough moment was when I was commissioned by the legendary Mary Portas [London's "Queen of the High Streets"] to do a public project at scale – the windows at Harvey Nichols [a department store in London] for London Fashion Week in 1997. I had an idea that was about the building itself, instead of just what was behind the glass. I wove one installation through the whole building. It won the Gold Award at the D&AD Design Awards for design, out of 27,000 entries. It was seen by all of London, and it was a radical idea.

↓ Passing on lessons learned

ASK YOURSELF WHY

It's really important to check your motivations. I've had people who say, "I want to be like you. I want to do what you do." And in a way, I do what I do not because I wanted to be a fancy designer, but because I saw problems. And in what I do, I'm trying to address problems that I perceive.

I think if your practice isn't driven at some level by societal issues, where you see a hole or a gap, but it's just about trying to be creative – I mean, I'm not trying to be creative, I'm trying to deal with problems. My goal was never to have a big studio with 250 people. I never dreamed I'd be doing this. I never thought we'd get these opportunities. I assumed I would be working in obscurity, but I was committed to that. Because I knew that there was a thing that mattered, where success or failure didn't matter. I didn't expect success – I still don't. But I really enjoy striving. And I believe in it. And I know that's what I'm probably best at. So, I would urge people to not try to chase the outcome in terms of status, but to see where there is a gap in the world that you think you can fill with what you do. An outcome in terms of solving a problem, that's worth doing, committing your life to.

FINDING THE RIGHT MENTOR IS GAME-CHANGING

The person who went out of their way to help me, in an unexpected way, was Terence Conran – the designer, entrepreneur, business person, industrialist, person who revolutionised food in Britain, retailing in Britain and influenced the founding of IKEA with his business, Habitat. He was at my university, and I had the fortune of being able to tap him on the shoulder when he was going out through the fire exit and ask his advice about something. I knew this person understood not just design, but how you get design to people. He turned around and said, "Come and see me".

TAKEAWAY

It's so important to continually research your industry including all the key trends, thinking, events and players. As to the latter, you can start to identify the people you admire the most and that you may see as important role models. This sets you up to be able to speak to them if the opportunity arises, which it often will.

I went expecting to spend five minutes with him, but he spent three hours with me, and even ended up saying I could live at his house! He enabled me to be able to pursue some ideas that were stuck and that might not have been able to happen otherwise. He became a lifelong friend and inspiration for me. He made space for me at that fledgling stage when my confidence was fragile, and gave me the benefit of the doubt, and I had the chance to grow and learn because of that.

Marketing

Marketing is the art and science of letting the world know about your brand, and demonstrating why they should love it.

It's about telling your brand story in the most compelling way over the most effective channels to reach your target audience, with a view to engaging them and turning them into loyal repeat customers and ideally brand advocates.

Below is an overview of the key topics you need to know about marketing your brand to the world.

Start with a simple marketing plan

Create yours by answering the following questions:

Who is your target audience and where can you find them?
Everything you do should revolve around your customers, so getting to know them is essential from the beginning. Create "personas" of your customers, detailed descriptions of everything you know and can imagine about them, e.g. which social media they use, their age range and lifestyle, where they live, what media brands they engage with, which other brands they love and where they shop.

What platforms will you use and how are you going to measure success?
Building on the persona work above, determine the platforms that resonate most with your target audiences and also feel authentic to your brand. Start by focusing on just one or two. Consider which metrics are most important for your business, so you can measure the effectiveness of specific campaigns. Audience growth? Engagement? Conversion? This will inform the direction of your marketing time, energy and budget.

What type of content will you share and when?
What exactly will your brand story look like on an ongoing basis across different platforms, including your newsletter and social

media? Plan your content strategy ahead of time. An easy way to organise the types of content you'll share is to apply it across the four standard "core content pillars": promotional, entertainment, educational and conversational. Create a document with a column for each content pillar and plan which content to share on which platforms in which timeframes.

Prepare your website

This is your home, where your brand lives and where you'll drive traffic from your marketing activities. Before launching your marketing activities, your website must be ready to handle traffic coming in from all channels, and provide a great user experience.

You also need to set up your website analytics, so you can gauge which of your web pages are most popular, how your customers navigate across your site, and which marketing channels drive the most traffic and conversions.

Key Marketing channels

Like most things, marketing is all about priorities. Of the myriad of marketing channels available, below are highlights of the top priority channels you should be familiar with.

1. Word of mouth

This is the most important channel, as nothing matches having a customer directly tell others that your brand is fantastic. The most powerful way to build word-of-mouth marketing is with direct connection with your brand, you as the founder and your team. First and foremost, this is where you put your personal network to work. Make sure your list of contacts is up to date and email them about launches and key news. Invite them to engage with any sales, events or other activities you are engaged in and ask them to sign up to your newsletter. As these are people already in your personal network, they'll be the most likely to want to support you and your business.

2. Email marketing

This is the second most important channel, as it means you have a direct relationship with someone via their email address. Creating a newsletter will be key, as it's an easy way to keep up regularly with your audience. Besides getting sign-ups via your personal network, you should also use your social media channels, website and any events (online or IRL) to drive sign-ups to your newsletter.

You should also segment your email list, so you can send targeted emails to various groups.

3. Social media marketing

Social media is a highly effective channel for connecting your brand directly with your target audience For creative start-ups especially, it's a great way to tell your brand story directly, your way.

To encourage engagement, use eye-catching visuals and attention-grabbing copy. There's no magic formula; you need to experiment to see what works best. Once you experiment with organic marketing and begin to understand what works and what doesn't, you can start experimenting with paid social media marketing.

Social media carries even more relevance if you're selling products online, as it's tied to e-commerce. With shoppable posts and in-app purchasing the norm, start-ups can directly influence consumer choices and make sales.

4. Public Relations (PR)

PR is getting your messaging out through journalists writing for media platforms. The power of PR is that it constitutes an endorsement of your brand from a third party as opposed to you generating positive messaging about yourself (in traditional terms, known as "earned" vs "owned"). You can also significantly increase your awareness via the reach of the media platform the journalist uses. The keys to getting PR are researching and getting to know journalists most likely to cover your brand and fine-tuning the angle of your message to fit what they write about.

If you're new to PR, it's natural to feel a bit daunted, especially when it comes to contacting journalists. But remember: they need you as much as you need them. Their success depends on writing about the most interesting, useful and innovative products and brands, so you're helping them out by giving them a good story.

↓ Tips for creating emails people will read

- To boost engagement, create unique newsletters with eye-catching, personalised subject lines and relevant content.
- Always include a call-to-action (CTA), such as, "Sign up for this event". Make it clear and prominent.
- Use emails to announce important happenings. The right emails at the right time will get the most returns.

↓ Tips on how to work with journalists

- Research the publication and the journalist. Understand their audience. What types of stories do they cover? What do they deem newsworthy?
- Map out your story. What's your angle? What's new or interesting? Why are you telling the journalist about this now?
- Write a press release or pitch, and prepare your visual assets.
- Tailor your approach (no mass, anonymous emails).
- Follow up with your contacts and try to build genuine relationships.
- Make sure to respond promptly to any questions. Journalists are the ultimate influencer, so they deserve respect.

C

MATTHEW SLOTOVER

The Art Market Visionary

3

Matthew Slotover
Co-founder of Frieze

It's the late 1980s, and everyone knows that New York is the centre of gravity of contemporary art – always has been, always will be. London, in particular, is known as a contemporary art backwater. But something has been quietly ticking away at Goldsmiths College of Art in southeast London. The artist Michael Craig-Martin was a teacher at Goldsmiths then – I'll let him tell you the rest of the story...

Michael Craig-Martin recounts...

In the early 70s, Goldsmiths had merged all departments – painting, sculpture, printmaking, film, video, performance – into one fine art department. Here, each student was expected to choose how they wished to work, but also change medium at will. This unusual level of control helped them become accustomed to taking full responsibility for their work.

In the summer of 1988, Damien Hirst, still a second-year student, curated "Freeze" – an ambitious exhibition of recent student work in a derelict east London warehouse. Damien invited me to see it the day before it opened and I was blown away. Its success owed much to his exceptional entrepreneurship. All the artists in Freeze had been students at Goldsmiths – Gary Hume, Fiona Rae, Mat Collishaw, Sarah Lucas, Michael Landy and Ian Davenport. The comprehensively high quality and maturity of the work of these very young artists attracted immediate attention in the London art world and quickly spread internationally.

It became the start of a movement and the Goldsmiths students were soon joined by their peers from other schools: Rachel Whiteread, Tracey Emin and others. Freeze spawned other warehouse exhibitions, giving this new generation of artists direct access to their ever-growing audience. It became clear that a life-changing opportunity had opened up for these budding artists, creating the circumstances necessary to establish sustainable careers.

At the time, simple survival was the aim: the idea of big money and fame were just distant dreams. It was a moment of youthful

↓ Matthew Slotover: Highlights

- Studied Psychology at Oxford University
- Launched *Frieze* magazine in 1991
- Launched Frieze Art Fair in London in 2003
- Launched Frieze Masters 2011, a meeting of contemporary art and old masters
- Launched Frieze New York 2011, Frieze LA 2019, Frieze Seoul 2022
- Opened first permanent exhibition and events space at 9 Cork Street London 2021

↑ Over 290 galleries from all over the world display their work at Frieze in London's Regent's Park

exuberance and innocence. They would become known as "The Young British Artists", the "YBAs". As I say in my book, *On Being An Artist*, in the art world of today, an artist needs to act like an entrepreneur in ways that 30 years ago most would not have considered.

Into this hotbed of late '80s London warehouse exhibitions enters a new university graduate who never liked art, Matthew Slotover. A friend of his, who studied art at Central Saint Martins, takes him to one of these early shows and he is astounded. He's never seen art like this, nor heard art talked about like this. He is captivated and wants to know everything about it.

The obvious place to look is art magazines. But he finds the ones that exist to be badly written, poorly designed and that they don't talk about the art he is interested in. He'd done a magazine at university and had always loved design and photography, so he thought, *Hey – I'll do a magazine*. That was the beginning of *Frieze*. The cover of the inaugural issue featured a Damien Hirst butterfly painting.

And the "YBAs"? They took the world by storm and London soon became, by many measures, the centre of the contemporary art world.

This status was cemented further by Matthew and his co-founder Amanda Sharp when they started Frieze Art Fair in 2003, which disrupted the art world again and quickly established itself as the key event for all major players in contemporary art. It's not an overstatement to say that, with these inventions, Matthew has single-handedly reinvented the contemporary art world.

I spoke to Matthew at the Serpentine Gallery in London.

Starting *Frieze* magazine

When I arrived in London in the late 1980s with my new university degree in psychology, I was casting around for what I wanted to do with my life. There weren't many jobs around then, as 1989 was deep in the throes of recession, and I couldn't do anything with my psychology degree, as I didn't want to be a psychologist. So when I started going to all of these amazing YBA shows in London and got interested in starting an art magazine, I was thrilled and started looking into how to set up a magazine and make it work.

Initially, I thought I'd find a sponsor who'd pay for everything – but of course, no one was going to sponsor it. Ironically, although I come from a family of entrepreneurs, I realised I didn't

↖ Michael Craig-Martin, the highly influential conceptual artist instrumental in fostering the Young British Artists movement while a teacher at Goldsmiths

↑ "Away from the Flock" by Damien Hirst, consisting of a lamb preserved in formaldehyde in a steel and glass vitrine

← Matthew Slotover and Amanda Sharp, co-founders of *Frieze*

know much about business, so I did a short business course and a short magazine-production course.

TAKEAWAY Even though we know it's logically not the case, when building your own business it can feel as though you're expected to know everything. "Part of being an entrepreneur is that you just figure things out" is a common refrain. While there may be truth in this generalised concept, to state the obvious: no one can know everything. Stay focused on what your skill sets are and be open to making the judgement that, in some circumstances, it's far more time and cost efficient to invest in expert help via a course or paid advice from an expert after you've exhausted your own resources to figure things out through your own research or network.

My *Frieze* co-founder Amanda Sharp and I had some mentors, including a designer and a writer who'd both been involved in some big art magazines. They introduced us to lots of people and steered us away from some bad ideas. About a year and a half after having the initial idea, the first issue of *Frieze* came out.

A stroke of luck

The magazine launched in a very modest way – the first issue had 32 pages and we printed 500 copies. But it had the first-ever published interview with Damien Hirst, who was on the cover, and people seemed to like it. There was a big art magazine around at the time called *Artscribe* which had been going for 15 years. By

← Frieze Art Fair London
  in Regents Park

a fluke of timing, they had a disastrous relaunch just as we were launching. A new owner had raised the price of *Artscribe* to £10 and made it big and fancy, which wasn't what people wanted, and it folded six months later. Everyone said, "Okay, you're the new *Artscribe!*" So we kind of inherited all their writers, readers and advertisers – which was a stroke of luck.

Timing is so important. Had I not been born in 1968 and graduated in 1989, I'd have missed a moment in British art that hasn't been repeated since. There was a kind of electricity in the air. Someone would do something amazing one week and someone else would do something even more amazing the next. Partly it was luck, and partly it was recognising what was going on.

TAKEAWAY

While you can't manufacture luck, or replicate someone else's, you can put yourself in a position to harness luck when it comes your way. The key is to become as expert as possible in your chosen sector, including by reading and researching as widely as possible and by getting to know about the key players and hopefully meeting as many of them as possible. This will not only put you in a position to jump on opportunities armed with your deep sector knowledge, but will also hone that intangible skill which Matthew notes is the ability to "recognise what is going on."

Gut instinct

We were living with our parents when we started. We didn't have an overdraft; we just spent whatever money was coming in. After the first issue, we got some Arts Council funding and the Lisson Gallery in London took the ad on the back page from the second issue onwards. It took about seven years before we had enough staff and could pay them a market salary. It was a slow "overnight success".

As it would happen, the timing of the first Frieze Art Fair turned out to be just right, too. We'd always had a soft spot for art fairs. In the early 1990s, we'd fill a car with our magazines and drive to fairs in Europe to see the art and meet the artists, critics, curators and dealers. We couldn't help noticing that Paris, Cologne, Brussels and Madrid all had art fairs – and that Italy had three. Every city except London seemed to have one – which wasn't so surprising, as London was a bit of a backwater then, without many galleries or collectors.

As the 1990s went on, Londoners got more interested in contemporary art and people started bringing their collecting habits to the capital. As the city became more internationalised, we thought, "Well, someone's got to do an art fair here," which grew into, "Maybe we should do it." We saw that other big magazine companies in other sectors also did events. It makes sense, as the readers of your magazine are the same people who visit your events – and the advertisers in your magazine are the exhibitors at your events. So although an art fair is a large, physical event, it's not so different from a magazine.

We saw that while art fairs are about buying and selling, the vast majority of art fair visitors have no intention of buying. They're just there to look at the art and also to bump into people. We saw that art fairs are also social events and fun. So we looked at how we could create a great experience for visitors by looking at things we disliked about existing fairs – like the feeling of walking into an exhibition centre and seeing stand after stand showing similar things.

First, we thought a lot about where the fair would be. We knew people love parks, which are obviously public spaces, and thought the "fair in a tent in a park" format would be great. We got the rights to do it in Regents Park and that turned out to be a big plus with our visitors, as well as setting us apart from other art fairs. And we also livened it up by bringing in great architects to design the space and also commissioning artists to do special projects. We also brought in great restaurants to do pop-ups, which proved to be very popular.

And despite not knowing much about the trends in the art market or the stock market, we instinctively felt it was a good time in the economy. Frieze launched its first fair in 2003 in Regents Park.

Our overall philosophy with the fairs (as with the magazine) was:

 The art comes first. If the art is good, everything else will follow.

We weren't inventing anything new with either the magazine or the fair. It's really difficult to invent a new model, but you can often tweak one if you spot how it can be done better.

↑ The first issue of *Frieze*
magazine from 1991, the
cover featuring a work by
Damien Hirst

Growing with the flow

After the Lehman Brothers bankruptcy in 2008, we thought, *This is going to be disastrous – it could be the end of everything.* But our fair worked quite well in 2009 and galleries were coming back in 2010. So, having survived a huge economic crisis, we felt the brand was robust enough to try something new.

The galleries had often said if we had a fair in New York, they'd love to do it. So we started exploring this option. We were approached by The Society of London Art Dealers on behalf of historical galleries, who needed a good space to show in. Alongside researching both these things, we spotted a gap in the market for a good German art magazine – so we looked into creating that too. And we thought, *Well, they're all goers – we should do all three. If we don't do them now, someone else might!* They all came to fruition at around the same time. We tripled our size in 18 months – I wouldn't recommend this!.

TAKEAWAY **This is a great illustration of the importance of following your instincts. Matthew considered both wider economic factors and more specific competitive factors, and decided, given all the information he had at the time, that pursuing all three opportunities at once was a good idea. So he took a risk and went for it and it turned out to be very successful. Resulting in an oft-repeated story: that if an entrepreneur knew at the time how daunting a project actually was, they'd never had taken it on – but because they didn't know at the time, they persevered and it ended up being something groundbreaking.**

Getting the backing

We never knew what money we had coming in for the magazine, as the advertising varied from issue to issue, but we avoided risk by never spending more than we had in the bank. With the fairs, our magazine customers had said in advance they'd like to participate, so the revenue was always there. But we were starting to hit the limit of what we could do. We had loads of ideas, but they involved a level of risk we didn't want to take.

We weren't actively thinking about sponsorship, but one night in 2016 someone deliberately sat me next to a guy called Ari Emanuel, head of major Hollywood talent agency William Morris Endeavor, at a private dinner in London, because they knew he was a fan of Frieze. Ari asked me about the money side of things and he said, "We could get you much more than that. Let us do it for you." For us, William Morris Endeavor was a dynamic company who were doing really interesting things in music, TV, film, fashion, sport, food – pretty much everything except art. So we eventually ended up agreeing to their taking a major stake in Frieze. We were excited to learn from all those other areas and felt like kids in a candy store.

Their sponsorship hasn't dramatically changed the culture of Frieze – we're still the same people in the same office. But it gives us opportunities and options. If we need to do something that's going to cost a lot of money, we can now do it. More than that, it's the sharing of knowledge, resources and expertise. We can say, "We're thinking about such and such," and they're like "Yeah, talk to our person in fashion...".

↓ Frieze New York opened in 2017, at iconic cultural centre "The Shed" in Manhattan's Hudson Yards, in the Chelsea gallery district adjacent to the High Line

Is "us" a plus or a minus?

Amanda Sharp joined me at *Frieze* magazine right back in the beginning in July 1991 and she and I co-founded the art fair in 2003. We've been friends since we were 18 and have very similar tastes, backgrounds and judgement. But we're different as well. Amanda's more salesy, and I'm more operations. Essentially, she makes the money and I spend it.

Although we have complementary skills and roles, there's a lot of business in the middle we both need to agree on. This is sometimes an issue.

> When we're arguing about big things, it's exciting – we're passionate about finding the best solution and learning from each other.

But if we're arguing over tiny things, it's just a fight – like sibling rivalry. It's uncomfortable for the rest of the staff to see us being mean to each other over something pathetic. Separating our roles has helped a lot and every time we start getting into that territory, we define our jobs more clearly and say, "Okay, you take this part, I'll take this part."

↓ Frieze Los Angeles launched in 2019 at Paramount Movie Studios

↓ Passing on lessons learned

ORIGINALITY

I don't really believe there's an original idea. I think ideas are the confluence of two other ideas, making a third. So everything we've done is really stolen from other people, but done in a new format. A couple of years before we launched Frieze Art Fair, "100% Design" held their interior design fair in a tent on King's Road and I asked the guy who created it if he'd recommend that approach. He said, "Yeah, it's much better – you have your own venue, you can use architects..." So we stole that idea for the art world where no one had really done it before – so in that sense, it was new. You've got to steal from the right places.

STEPPING BACK

You can have moments of doubt in contemporary art. If you go to a few shows that aren't good and you see the same things coming around again, you can worry you're going to lose interest. But this only tends to last until you see something amazing and get re-energised by it. When you're deep in operation, it can drag you down and you can get too close. I haven't had that for a long time, partly because I'm not so operational now. I can step back and just go and see more shows.

PURPOSE

A really good employee left us a few years ago, and during her exit interview, Amanda was telling her about the origins of Frieze. The woman said, "If I'd known all of that, I never would have left." And we thought, "Wow – we must communicate better to our staff about what drives us." So now, we always take time to tell new starters how it all began and what it's all about.

I sometimes look at the very first issue of our magazine. It had a clean design, it had interviews, special projects, young artists, older artists, things that weren't art... and it still has all those things. It hasn't changed dramatically. It's got bigger. It's got more international. And now it comes out on time.

Investors

Getting an investor can be the best thing that ever happened to your business – or the worst. Or something in between. Or you may not need one at all.

Looking at the mainstream conversation around entrepreneurship today, you might conclude that every business needs investors in order to succeed. This might be true for the high-stakes tech sector, but it isn't the case for all sectors.

 Getting an investor is like getting married – don't do it lightly.

Carolyn Dailey

The key thing to realise is that when an investor invests by buying shares in your company, they become a part-owner alongside you. If you do decide to go down this route, it's important to have a full understanding of investor expectations and their potential impact.

What investors want – the bottom line

An investor's agenda is very simple. They invest a sum of money in a company in order to make a multiple of that amount in return, within a fixed period of time – that's it. No matter what else is said, done or implied, that is the bottom line. Knowing this will give you a guiding North Star and hopefully help you avoid any possible misunderstandings.

Different types of investors

An initial funding avenue is to approach family and friends for investment. But this is only a possibility for a small percentage of founders surrounded by a network offering that kind of support. Clearly, there are risks involved with mixing money and personal relationships, too.

Next come **angel investors**. These are generally high net worth individuals who invest in start-ups using their own personal funds. They can shoulder more risk than investors who use other people's money, and tend to be motivated by a passion for new ideas and for helping new founders grow their businesses. If they know what they're doing (it's up to you to do your background research), they will understand that at an early investment stage a business needs flexibility to experiment and test the market, so they will be largely sympathetic to that, and often encourage it.

Venture Capital investors, or VCs, get money from outside investors, which they normally pool with their own money, to invest large sums into start-ups that show great growth potential. If your business plan includes exponential growth, this could be the perfect avenue for you – but you'll be working against the clock to hit VC targets.

Private Equity investors are similar to VCs, but they come in at a later stage. They should be called on when the business is substantially developed, but still shows high growth potential. It is normally the last round of investment before a company goes public.

The investor relationship

This is a unique and deeply human relationship; not only do the numbers have to be just right but, like the marriage, the chemistry does, too.

Just as there are all kinds of creative founders, there are all kinds of investors out there. If you feel investment is the right path for you, the key is to find an investor who completely "gets" you and your business; someone you feel very comfortable with and who you feel is in your corner.

Do your research. Find out everything about the investor's background, expertise and connections. Find out which other businesses they've invested in, and if possible, ask those founders how their experience has been.

Finally, be extremely clear about how the relationship will work and what the expectations are on both sides. It's crucial that you are able to discuss these issues honestly and openly, and that they are clearly conveyed in your stock purchase agreement.

C

RUTHIE ROGERS

The Alchemist of Cuisine

Ruthie Rogers
Founder of The River Cafe

It's the late 1980s and Ruthie Rogers has just moved back to London from Paris, where she has been living with her husband, the architect Richard Rogers, while he built the Pompidou Centre. She's a graphic designer by trade, but decides to turn her hand to food. There's a tiny space within the compound of formerly dilapidated warehouses which Richard has converted into offices filled with architects and designers in west London on a bend in the River Thames. They'd put out a call for applications to open a cafe there, but none seemed quite right. So Ruthie, with no experience in restaurants but a burning passion for them, decided to open a cafe herself.

Fast forward 30 years, and that tiny cafe has become The River Cafe, the iconic Michelin-starred Tuscan restaurant considered by many to be the best Italian restaurant in the world, as unlikely as that may seem for a restaurant in London. It's also a majorly successful business, complemented by a huge publishing business based on The River Cafe cookbooks.

All aspects of the business are going from strength to strength – and then the pandemic strikes. Like all restaurants, The River Cafe has to close.

What to do next? If you're Ruthie Rogers, you pivot and start new creative businesses to serve and delight your community.

The first is an e-commerce business. While scrambling, like everyone, to work out which end is up and how to protect her staff, Ruthie realises they have a lot of longer-life stock like pastas, jars of tomatoes and cheeses. So she starts a website where they can sell these online. In true Ruthie style, she makes sure the website has beautiful design and photography. She then realises The River Cafe's fish buyers and butchers are struggling to sell their products, so she adds them to the website. She then expands the online shop to include design products – for example, lamps designed by Norman Foster, bowls designed by John Pawson and flower vases designed by Zaha Hadid. The shop goes mega. She supplements the website with a newsletter, letting people

↗ The River Cafe interior
with its open kitchen,
beloved clock and pink
pizza oven

↓ Ruthie Rogers: Highlights

- Born and raised in upstate New York
- Came to study in London for her second year of university in 1968
- Met and married Richard Rogers, and moved to Paris, where he built the Pompidou Centre
- Started The River Cafe in 1979 with her friend Rose Gray

- Started her publishing business in 1995 with the launch of the first The River Cafe cookbook
- Received a Michelin Star in 1997
- Started an e-commerce business in 2020
- Launched a podcast in 2021

know what The River Cafe is doing week by week. It becomes a great connector, a way to bring The River Cafe back to the people they've missed so much. When lockdown is over, people have been buying things from the website and reading the newsletter, so there's a great continuity that takes The River Cafe to even greater heights.

The next new business she invents during lockdown is a podcast, called Ruthie's Table 4 (referring to her favourite table at The River Cafe). She thought of it as a way to stay in touch with The River Cafe community and a wider audience. At first, she imagines asking guests to read a recipe every day – her feeling being that a recipe is part poetry and part science, and that they're actually rather beautiful to listen to. But her friend Graydon Carter (founder of *Airmail Weekly* and former editor of *Vanity Fair*), says, "Come on Ruthie, It has to be more than that."

So her idea evolves. Now, guests are invited onto the show to recall their food memories, which are often visceral and personal. For example, recalling family suppers, first dates, what they eat when they're performing, what they eat when they need comfort. As she says, "Food is politics, food is cultural, food is how you express love, food is about your heritage, it defines who you are and who you want to be." From its simple beginnings, the podcast has become a big hit, with guests ranging from Paul McCartney, Wes Anderson and Emily Blunt, to David Beckham, Austin Butler and Es Devlin.

I spoke to Ruthie at her home in London.

The beginnings

I was born in upstate New York in the middle of the Catskill Mountains. My parents moved to Woodstock when I was about 12 and that was a radical change for me. It was a town that had its roots in art and painting. Bob Dylan bought a house there around 1963, and that radically changed the town into much more of a music place. It was 100 miles from New York City, but a very stimulating and lovely place to grow up. It was the 1960s, and there was the Vietnam War and my parents were quite socially minded and involved in peace movements. We grew up with a sense of social participation and giving back to society.

I moved to London as a student in about 1968. I'd studied in Colorado and then Vermont – it was a bit too much "country" for me, so my parents let me take my second year of university in London when I was about 19 years old. I loved being in London and wanted to stay, as the times were very exciting with the student movements around the Vietnam War in London, Paris and Berlin – I was hungry for a political and social environment.

My parents said I could only stay if I continued with university, so I went to the London College of Printing and got my BA in graphic design. And that turned into my being here for more than 50 years.

I met Richard Rogers just before he won the competition for the Pompidou Centre in Paris with Renzo Piano. By that time, I had finished school and was working at Penguin Books in the art department. Richard went to Paris to work on the competition and I stayed in London and we lived between the two. We never thought that building would happen. But then it became clear that it was going to happen, so we moved to Paris in about 1972.

Paris and the Pompidou

Living in Paris was a huge influence on me in every way – to be watching the creation of such an exciting building and to be living with people who were so international, coming from California, Italy and London to work on the Pompidou Centre. We were all there together doing one thing and I started working in the office with Richard.

 I always say, part of that whole adventure was the food.

← Ruthie and her husband, architect Sir Richard Rogers

We ate out every weekend and every night during the week we had working meetings over meals. We always ate lunch at home because Renzo, being Italian, always wanted to come home for lunch, especially as his family weren't there.

So that's really when I started cooking. You see these amazing food markets in Paris and that's how you learn what's fresh and learn how seasonal the food is. When I was growing up, we had corn and strawberries in the summer and pumpkins in the winter. But it really hits you when you're in Paris; you go to get a melon, and they're all gone! They just aren't around anymore because it's the next season. That really taught me how to cook and how to shop.

Being there was also part of such an historical time. It was very brave of the French to let two young people – Richard was 38 and Renzo was 34, and they'd only completed 14 projects previously – create that iconic French landmark. They had an open international competition and nobody knew the jury (which included architectural heavyweights Oscar Niemeyer, Jean Prouvé and Philip Johnson) had selected Richard and Renzo's project until they opened the envelope. Everyone then learned it was an Italian (Renzo) and an Italian/British person (Richard) who'd won. The French had the courage to stick with the decision of the jury, despite the backlash they faced for not selecting French architects.

La Rentrée to London

After the Pompidou Centre was finished, we came back to London. Richard always knew that he wanted us to have an office that was part of a community, not just some space in an office building. Richard's partner was riding his bicycle one day and found a group of dilapidated warehouses in Hammersmith, on the river Thames. They had great open space and light and so Richard's practice bought them. They converted them into offices for themselves and also other designers and architects. Being outside of Central London, there was no place to eat. There was space for a cafe, so we put out a call out for applications for people to run one. Looking at the applications that came in, there just weren't any that were right.

We said to each other, "You know, the only thing worse than not having somewhere to eat would be having a mediocre one." So we said, "Why don't we do it ourselves?"

And my next call was to Rose Gray. I'd known Rose for years. She was a great domestic cook and was also doing some cooking at restaurants in London. We went and looked at the site and said, "Let's do it!"

TAKEAWAY **It's important to be aware of your skills, background and passions so that when opportunities arise, you're ready to recognise when they fit and you can harness them. These may be outside your comfort zone, but if you're secure in what your goals are, you're in a position to grab the opportunity and take a calculated risk based on what you know you're capable of and passionate about.**

There were big challenges. First of all, it was hard to get to. Nobody knew where it was (except the taxi drivers because it was part of the Knowledge!). And because it's in a residential neighbourhood, when we first opened we could only be open at lunch on Monday to Friday, and only for the people who worked in the warehouses, so as not to attract cars to the neighbourhood. So it was very, very basic and made no money at all.

We had only nine tables. One day, Rose would make a pasta and I'd do the sandwich and then the next day she'd do the sandwich and I'd make the pasta. But those restrictions, for two women who really didn't have much experience at all in restaurants or cooking or business, were really a fantastic thing because, in hindsight, it gave us time to find our feet.

← Ruthie with her The River Cafe co-founder Rose Gray

→ "Shop The River Cafe",
the e-commerce site
Ruthie started during
the pandemic to
maintain the connection
with The River Cafe
clients, has continued,
expanding from food and
drink to homeware,
including lamps
designed by architect
Norman Foster

From the beginning, we always set out to run it as a business. There were three factors that were key to us to start with. First, we were small. Second, Richard funded us – but only with £25,000, that's what we built the restaurant on. We could do it because we kept our overheads to the bare minimum – I went to the Reject Shop to buy table settings, Rose went to the north of England to buy second-hand grills and ovens.

And third, Richard gave us his accountant, so we could learn the basics of that side. I always said that if I had an espresso at the restaurant, I would pay for the espresso. If somebody took home a pound of cabbage, they'd pay: we were really, really careful. I do think that you can be friendly, you can be generous, you can let staff take food home, but everything has to be written down and everything has to be paid for. It's so crucial to have the help of an accountant in a business, and people don't often talk about that.

So there was never a huge surprise when we did our accounts, but we still lost money. Because, you know, we always wanted to use the best ingredients and we were competing with not another restaurant – as there were no other restaurants nearby – but with the sandwich shop selling the sandwiches, which obviously had lower costs.

TAKEAWAY

From the beginning, it's key to be clear on where you're aiming to head. This lets you plan a road map which you can then follow despite the ups and downs of the day-to-day business. For example, how much you're willing to spend over a range of years, how much revenue you can foresee coming in and, most of all, how quickly you want to grow.

The terrifying sommelier

In the late 1980s people in America and Britain – myself and people like Alice Waters (Chez Panisse in Berkeley California) and Wolfgang Puck (Los Angeles) – were all thinking about how restaurants could be different.

At the time, there were really only two choices for eating out: you either dressed up and were terrified of the sommelier and knowing which wine to order or you had a fantastic time at an informal place but didn't eat very well. We thought, *Why can't you eat well but still have fun?* So we were all thinking that way, with open kitchens and making pizzas, with no dress codes, having

sommeliers who weren't stuffy. The whole nature of restaurants started changing a lot then.

Growing the business

Over time The River Cafe started becoming known and we focused on growing the business, but we kept our growth very slow and careful. At first a lot of it was legal issues – we applied to be able to open for lunch to the public, then to be open for dinner, then to be open at the weekends (but only on Saturdays), and then to be open until midnight (vs. 10 p.m.) and then to be open on Sunday for lunch.

There's also been a lot of gentrification around us which has helped us grow. In the early days we once ordered a taxi for an American customer to go back to her hotel, and when we asked her where she was going, she said "London". There was a feeling you were at the end of the world. Now it seems easier to get to. And there are times now when we're absolutely packed and you go into the West End and the restaurants there aren't. So I think now people come to a destination restaurant.

We've never done traditional marketing, word just spread. People would come and tell their friends. And London is a very international city, so the word would easily spread to New York and LA and beyond.

Growing the space

Our original tiny cafe space eventually became too small. In 1994, additional space became available so we tore the whole thing apart. Richard designed the new space, we put in the stainless steel bar and we really felt like a proper restaurant then. Several years later, we got more space for a reception. Then, in 2008, we had a fire and had to close for six months. It was devastating. We could have just painted all the walls white and carried on but we decided to seize the opportunity and do something beautiful. We put in a private dining room, a cheese room and a completely open kitchen so there were no walls: everybody could see everyone else everywhere in the restaurant.

TAKEAWAY | **Sometimes the worst things that happen have a way of showing you a new way forward that leads to bigger visions and opportunities. No one likes setbacks, but when you have them (which is inevitable), think about what you can learn and how you can possibly re-frame your long-term goals.**

> For all of us, food is creative, political, intimate and most of all, an expression of community and love.

Ruthie Rodgers

The importance of design and creativity

Design has always been crucial to us – to me as a graphic designer, to Richard as an architect, and to Rose, who was an art teacher. I think for everyone, the things in your environment are crucial – the pots you use, your lighting (ours is by Renzo Piano). To us, it matters a lot. We wanted a space that was democratic, so there wasn't a good table or a bad table. Someone once came in and said, "What's your best table?" And I said, "Well, my husband likes to sit over there by the kitchen and Lucien Freud likes to sit by the door – you tell me what's the best table."

We love bright colours, so we love the blue carpet, the fuchsia pink wood pizza oven, the yellow hallway. We also love light and reflection. Richard designed the sloped windows that run all across the east wall so that they reflect the food that's on the bar when you look up and everyone can see what the chefs are cooking and the chefs can see all the people who are eating. It was all very important to us.

We also have a wonderful community of artists around us who started a tradition of drawing on our menus. The first was Ellsworth Kelly, who did a still life drawing of his table. Then Cy Twombly, Damien Hirst, Peter Doig, Brice Marden, Michael Craig-Martin and Ed Ruscha. So creativity and creators have always been very important to us.

↑ Exterior of The River Cafe, with its large dining area and garden over the River Thames

Managing team culture

I think the restaurant world has changed so much and the idea that people had to be taught through fear and bullying is really old-fashioned. The generation of young people who are working today just won't put up with it. And people who are in positions of responsibility don't want that behaviour in their restaurant. The culture of a restaurant should be no different from the culture of a newspaper or a law firm or a charity or any other professional organisation. For example, we have a lot of women working here – 50 per cent women in the restaurant, including great women chefs. We are all just doing our jobs.

When we started out we were tiny, so we could shape the culture from scratch. The great thing about working with Rose is that we very much shared the same values. I think that's very important, as you tend to have a shared vision and avoid some of the standard arguments. We both thought that we would treat the people who worked at The River Cafe a bit like we did our family when we were cooking at home. So everyone participated. Rose had an open kitchen, as do I and our children or guests always took part. It wasn't something where you had the kitchen miles away.

↓ The award-winning
  River Cafe cookbooks
  are a major part of its
  overall business, with
  the first published in
  1996 and multiple, highly
  successful follow-up books
  continuing to be released

The importance of rigour

I always shy away from too much talk about how "it's a family, family, family and we all love each other". There is that of course, and it underpins everything we do. But there has to be rigour, because people who are coming to us are spending money.

You have to make sure every inch of the restaurant is clean, that your apron is clean, that you don't shout in the kitchen. The person who's sitting near the kitchen should have every bit as much of a beautiful time as they would have in a restaurant where the kitchen is underground. They're just two different choices and I love going to both: to a restaurant that's open, like we have, and to one that's quiet, where you have no idea what's going on behind those doors.

And you never know if someone has saved up for months to come to us or if they've just had a bereavement in the family or if they're celebrating something. So our job is to make that experience happy and warm and what the person wants. Some people like engaging with the waiters, some people don't. It's really important that the whole team sense that. The people who work for us are sensitive to the people around them but also have the rigour. Sometimes you have to teach it more to some people and sometimes we end up learning from them.

Because, why do we engage with any business, including a restaurant? To be taken care of.

I always advise parents to have their children work in a restaurant because it teaches you a lot about what it means to be collaborative, responsible and nice – and to leave whatever you came in with. Same for me, I walk through those doors of The River Cafe, I might be troubled or worried about someone I love or something that's going on. But when you go through those doors you go into the mode of "We're on stage here" – the scripts have to be written, the sets have to be painted, the seats have to be clean, and the curtain goes up at 12.30 with expectations.

The Book Business

We love doing books. It's an extension of the restaurant but without having to open an additional physical site, which we've never felt comfortable with. We started with *The River Cafe Blue Book*, which I think was quite radical in the sense that we didn't have any food on the cover. We didn't have a food stylist: we made the food, put it on the table and it was photographed.
Then we had our friend Johnny Pigozzi take paparazzi-style photographs to give a feel for how the restaurant was. So that *Blue Book* was quite important.

After that we did the *Yellow Book*, which was about the wood oven and cooking at home, then the *Green Book*, which was mostly vegetables, then two *Easy Books* for people who just wanted to shop and cook. And then the *Classic Book*, which was the last book I did with Rose. We went to all the places in Italy where we'd learned our recipes. Then came *The River Cafe 30* which celebrated our 30th birthday and then the *Look Book* for kids. There were also small pocket books.

The Podcast Business

During lockdown, we started the podcast *Ruthie's Table 4*. The concept evolved into people's food memories. I think if I said to David Beckham, "Can we talk about football?", or to Paul McCartney, "Can we talk about the Beatles?", they might have done that. But if I say, "Can you just tell me, when you were growing up, did you sit down to family dinners, did your mom cook, did your dad cook, did you go out to restaurants?" That would be something really unique.

The things we've heard are fascinating. I find it particularly interesting that practically nobody we've interviewed grew up entitled. So, whatever their restrictions were, many people measure their success in whatever they were doing – as a musician and actor or a writer – by their ability to go out to a restaurant and order whatever they want. Or to learn about food or about wine.

Paul McCartney said that he thought wine was rubbish, because he'd only had really cheap wine. And when Brian Epstein took him out for a great meal, he realised that wine could be quite good. Rick Rubin, who's a music producer, had never eaten a meal at home because his parents took him out every night for fast food. Mel Brooks, who's 97, can remember the woman who first made him a pasta when he was eight years old. Food triggers so much: it's so deep and for all of us, it's so personal.

Ruthie's Podcast

Sharing what food means to
them, guests have included
David Beckham, Tina Fey,
Paul McCartney, Jony Ive,
Stanley Tucci, Austin Butler
and Es Devlin

↓ Passing on lessons learned

CONSIDER INVESTORS CAREFULLY
I don't think anybody goes into restaurants to
make millions. Well, maybe you do if you're going
to have a chain of 45 or whatever, but that's a
different business! Be really thoughtful about
whether to have investors and understand what
it means for your business. And if you decide to
have them, be thoughtful about the people you
have as investors. We always borrowed from the
bank, we didn't have investors. I think having
investors can be problematic – some people
have great investors and love working with them
but others have big problems, so it's something
to consider deeply.

START SMALL
For aspiring creative entrepreneurs, my biggest
piece of advice is to start small. I think that you
have to be really honest about what you have
and you don't have, so when times are getting
hard, you have to face them. If you don't face
things, then you can't deal with them. You can't
kid yourself that everything is going to be fine.

You have to look at your financial reality, whether
it's too many staff, costs that are too high or
wastage, or whatever. We put taking care of the
people who work for us as a very high priority.

LISTEN
I am surrounded by people who really help me
out. I can pick up the phone and call somebody
who knows everything about restaurants
or business or technology or just someone
I completely trust on life advice. So I think it's
crucial to choose the people around you carefully.
And then you listen to what they say and you
choose to either take their advice or leave it.
I don't always take it, but I listen.

Someone once asked me, "Who do you ask for
advice?" And I said, "I assume everyone knows
more than I do, so I go to everyone for advice.
It doesn't mean I always take it, but I listen."
Listening is probably my biggest piece of advice.

Team and Culture

It sounds like a cliché, but it's true – no one can do it all on their own. This is particularly the case when it comes to building a business. A huge range of skills are needed, and it's extremely rare, if not impossible, for one person to possess them all. So, it's vital that you find the right collaborators who can help you achieve your goals.

Understanding different types of collaborators and team members

Given mainstream conversation, you may think that "team member'"means "employee". But this is not the case. A whole range of people can be team members. The key distinction is their legal status vis-à-vis your company. An employee is a long-term member of the company, to whom the company makes many commitments and guarantees. Employees also come with tax and other costs which are at the expense of the company.

Employees vs. non-employee collaborators

Plenty of founders build highly successful teams without employing a single person in the early stages. A team doesn't have to represent numbers of employees on a payroll. It can also be a collection of people with diverse skills helping to grow your business. These are people who work on a fees-for-service basis such as freelancers, consultants and advisors who contribute to your skill base, reputation and revenue potential.

When is the right time to hire employees?

If you're starting out, it can be tempting to hire employees before you are truly ready. In fact you may get the impression from mainstream conversation – for example, various "top start-up" lists – that hiring employees quickly is a badge of honour, as start-ups are often judged as "successful" by the number of employees they have. At this stage of the entrepreneurial journey, your key concern should be to keep costs and commitments to a minimum, rather than bringing employees on board. The golden rule: only hire when you are making consistent money and you feel confident your business can benefit from and, crucially, afford an employee and keep your commitments to them.

Hiring your first employee is a big step. It comes with huge responsibilities and tax implications. You're now in charge of someone's livelihood, so don't take the decision lightly.

Bringing collaborators on board

Why "different" is good – expertise

Before bringing in collaborators, whether freelancers or employees, you need to be clear about your personal strengths and weaknesses. The more honest you are with yourself about your own skills and preferences, the easier it is to work out who to bring in to fill the gaps.

- Make a list of all the areas and tasks you love engaging with and are good at. These are things within your zone of genius that don't need outsourcing
- Now, list all the tasks you struggle with, don't have the skills for and don't enjoy

Don't battle away at things that don't come naturally. Instead, engage collaborators to take them off your hands, to do them better and faster, setting you free to do what you do best.

Why "same" is essential – values

While complementary skills are crucial, collaborators who share your values are essential. You could find stellar people with the exact expertise you need, but if you aren't aligned on the principles that matter most to your business, you're in for a difficult relationship. Always go back to your brand values.

How to attract top talent without big fees

As a start-up, you won't have the cachet or big budgets of a leading brand that everyone wants to work for. So, how can you attract the best collaborators? Luckily, people aren't always incentivised by financial gain alone. Key factors that can win them over include an inspiring mission and vision, engaging issues to work on, impressive people in your network to work with or a project that, if well-executed for you, will help them get future projects they're aiming for.

Touting for talent

Word-of-mouth remains the most successful way of connecting with potential collaborators. There's nothing like a personal recommendation, so approach your network and lean on your contacts.

Freelance sites like Upwork are also great, as they let you post very specific job descriptions and search for candidates based on very detailed criteria and evaluations. LinkedIn is also a great source for collaborators.

When reaching out to someone on LinkedIn, send a brief explanatory message, not a full job description. They'll look at your profile and respond if they're interested.

Building a culture

As a business leader, you need to think long and hard about the sort of culture you want to create and, importantly, to maintain. It comes down to the mission, vision and values you have defined and your own behaviour.

Day to day, as a founder, the most powerful way to encourage the right behaviour is to model it yourself. Get it right at the beginning, and you'll be surrounded by talented and loyal people for the long run.

A few things to consider on culture:
· Culture is your foundation. Nail it down at the start. Then live it
· Culture should reflect who you are and what your business stands for
· Culture should align with your business strategy and business plan
· All team members should be aware of the culture you are trying to create

Protecting your business

It's key to protect the business you've worked so hard to build. There are many issues that can cause serious problems if you don't put preventative measures in place. The most important is a rock solid standard freelance, consulting or employment contract (as applicable) that you've had checked by a lawyer. Key protections should include a specific description of services to be provided and money to be paid, confidentiality, IP, procedures if the relationship does not work out, discrimination and harassment policy. It's all too easy to think these things won't happen in your company, so be prepared.

C '

My passion is establishing the values
and culture that enable creative
business. It's about the relationships,
the realness, the ambitions,
the behaviours that unlock amazing
teams…and about continuous
experimentation and curiosity.

Matt "Mills" Miller, co-founder of ustwo games
creator of *Monument Valley*

C

STRAUSS
ZELNICK

The Games Master

Strauss Zelnick
Owner of Take-Two Interactive

When *Grand Theft Auto VI* is launched, it will be the biggest entertainment release of all-time, eclipsing any movie or music release. Bigger than the all-time record-breakers, James Cameron's *Avatar* and Michael Jackson's *Thriller*. I would wager that may come as a surprise. Most people outside the industry don't know that video games are by far the most commercially successful and fastest growing of all creative sectors. In fact, it's a $180bn business worldwide – bigger than movies, TV and music combined. Making a game takes longer and can cost more than making a blockbuster movie. At the high end, like *GTA*, they incorporate the best of creativity across all the sectors – from storytelling, music, choreography and design to art, animation and fashion.

What's more, video games are largely about community. Not only do they nurture an internal community of writers and designers, but they connect a network of highly active gamers around the world. This is a unique aspect of the video games sector; customers want to interact directly with each other, and see it as a key part of the product. Looking forward, video games already have their feet fully in the future: they've always been digital and have incorporated AI forever.

I spoke to Strauss at Take-Two Interactive's Headquarters in Midtown Manhattan.

↓ Strauss Zelnick: Highlights

- Started career at Columbia Pictures licensing TV internationally
- President and COO of 20th Century Fox – got them to No. 1 at the box office, from being last, under Rupert Murdoch and Barry Diller
- Greenlit *Dirty Dancing* – highest grossing independent film of all time

- Crystal Dynamics in 1993 – first exposure to video games – had a feeling video games would become the next big entertainment business
- 1995 – Recruited to BMG (Bertelsmann Music Group), to turn around one of the biggest music labels – went from No. 5 out of

6 to No. 2 out of 5 – "We'd have been No. 1 but No. 1 and 2 merged."

- Founded ZMC (Zelnick Media Capital) private equity
- Took over Take-Two (T2) in 2007
- After EA (Electronic Arts), T2 is the world's No. 2 pure play interactive company
- ZMC owns Second City Comedy Club in Chicago; alums include most of the *Saturday Night Live* cast

↑ *Grand Theft Auto VI*, due to drop in 2025, is one of the most highly anticipated game releases in history

Taking over Take-Two Interactive

When we took over Take-Two (T2) in 2007, it was a pretty troubled company. The Chairman had been indicted, the CFO and the company itself were under investigation by the authorities, including the SEC, the IRS and the New York District Attorney's Office. It hadn't filed its financial statements, hadn't had its annual meeting, had fired its auditors, was losing a bunch of money and had very little capital left. It was on the brink of bankruptcy.

But we saw that there was exceptional creative talent at T2, so there was an opportunity for the creation of hits. Our view was that if we could just restructure the company so that it ran sensibly and convince the creative talent to stay and give them the freedom and security to pursue their passion, I thought we would do well. And we did.

Rockstar Games – a key talent at T2 and a rich history

A mega talent we saw at T2 was Rockstar Games, the creator of *GTA*, and there was a great history there. I was CEO at BMG (Bertelsmann Music Group, one of the major music labels). While there I founded BMG Interactive – turns out Sam Houser was an intern there – he's a lot younger! He founded Rockstar Games at BMG Interactive and created *Grand Theft Auto*. BMG Interactive was then sold to T2 in 1998. So, for me, buying T2 in 2007, everything came full circle from the BMG Interactive days. An example of what set Rockstar apart from the beginning is that

they don't see themselves as a games company but as a "cultural brand." They do marketing arguably better than anyone else – do their demos in a space kitted out as the ultimate gamer's room. And they really encourage their teams to bring in all of their creative and cultural interests across the sectors.

Creating a space where creatives can do their best work

For me, the top priority is to create an environment where creators can pursue their passions. I don't see a trade-off between big budgets and creative freedom. We know what it costs to make a game. You then have to bet on the best creators and insist – not just encourage, but *insist* – that they pursue their passions, and that's what creates hits.

On the business side, we try to run a very efficient, rational business that's ambitious and seeks excellence and also insists that people behave in a respectful manner, with kindness to one and other, because that frees people up to do their best work and to come up with great ideas.

Three part strategy

We've been saying this for 17 years in every private and public communication. It's not just saying it; you have to be consistent with strategy for it to be meaningful, and we are.

Be the most creative: Meaning, hire the best creators and *insist* they pursue their passions. Encourage them to always try something new and to stay away from derivative and copy-cat works. In Hollywood it's common to pitch your product as "It's a combination of *Spiderman* meets *Batman* meets *Back to the Future*." We don't do that here; we want something that you've never seen before.

The biggest hits in every form of entertainment – and I've been in every form – are, by their nature, unexpected. This is why I'm not worried about AI creating hits, because it's built on data that already exists. It's backward-looking. Big hits are forward-looking and therefore need to be created out of thin air.

Being the most creative means not just thinking outside the box; it means there is no box.

← Gamers attending the Electronic Entertainment Expo play a demo of *Borderlands* from Take-Two Interactive

Be the most innovative: Meaning, in every part of your business, don't just think today or tomorrow, but think years ahead and try to propel the creative and strategic sides of the business forward on

that basis. It involves taking enormous risks and spending a lot of money on things that don't work out. So, it's not at odds with creativity, but maybe at odds with efficiency. It would be way easier to say we're just based on creativity and efficiency. But as we're in a technology-driven business, if we're not constantly innovating, we'll be left behind.

For example, Rockstar was the first company to release downloadable content with *GTA IV*.

Be the most efficient: Meaning, run a tight ship – be compliant, be ethical, make rational decisions in short order, have good customer service, take care of your colleagues so the trains run on time. If you go to an office and there are cardboard boxes in the reception area and the bathrooms are dirty, that tells you a lot about the company.

Starting your own video game company requires big funding and lots of people

The days of starting a games company with a few friends in your garage are long gone. It takes a lot of capital, a lot of time and a lot of people – it's very hard to do. Even the Housers, who started Rockstar Games, started at a big company, BMG. You can't just get together with your friends and start an independent video game company unless you're prepared to have no income for three to five years and somehow manage to field a team of a couple hundred people during that time.

In terms of investing ourselves in games studios, we look at what they've done before and what they're working on now, as you would in any industry. Where we're positioned at T2, it's not like we pluck people out of obscurity, give them a bunch of money and hope for the best. We work in the major leagues, with established creators who have done great things before – they must have worked in the minor leagues before they get to us.

We do have a division that's focused on new independent projects, called Private Division, working with creators with less experience, but typically not with no experience. For people with no experience, they generally need to get experience working at other studios.

AI

Generative AI will be really important to many businesses including ours. We've had AI tools here forever – T2 has been a leader in AI, not just in this company, but in the industry. I don't think that will change.

But those who think you can push a button and say: "Create the next *GTA VI* and make it bigger and better, here's all the code and the marketing plan", you're not going to get anything you can work with. Because it's a combination of massive data sets, large language models and computing – and all of that, as I said, is backward-looking. What comes out is a predictive model. Some of the stuff we do can be predictive, but the really creative stuff can't be. The big creative leaps forward will be generated by humans.

Automation will replace mundane routine jobs and free up humans to do more interesting stuff, but humans will always be needed for more complex tasks. Automation and technology will take us to higher and higher levels over time because they always have.

Networking

What is networking?

That's obvious, right? It's a socially acceptable way to use people. And also a soul-destroying activity requiring you to have forced, inauthentic conversations with people you would otherwise not want to connect with.

This isn't true. Networking can be inspiring and fulfilling, but unfortunately the term has accumulated such awful connotations over the years that it fills everyone with dread.

The activity we're actually talking about is one of the most enjoyable parts of building your business because it's all about people. About getting to know all kinds of different people, learning about their interests, world views, lessons, tips and fears. It's about building relationships with people who are on the same journey as you are. So, apologies for the label, but let's dig into the essentials of effective networking.

Why is networking essential?

By building a network, you are essentially building a community around you. If done well and authentically, it will provide you with information, advice, support, opportunities and, perhaps most importantly, camaraderie with like-minded people.

More specifically you will:
- Learn about what's out there – in terms of competition, mentors who have been there before, challenges that might lie ahead, possible suppliers or new customers, etc.
- Find out more about yourself by talking to others and refine your business ideas
- Get advice and top tips from those in the know
- Link up with potential business collaborators
- Meet possible mentors who could guide you in future
- Secure new customers, clients or contracts from key discussions

How to network successfully

1. Define your vision
- Find your North Star – where do you see yourself at the height of what you define as success? Use this to guide your networking journey
- Who inspires you? Which entrepreneurs do you look up to and admire?
- Make a mood board to give your vision a visual focus

2. Research your target market
- Who are the key players?
- Where do they hang out? (Follow them on social media, read trade publications, sign up for newsletters, set Google alerts, attend meet-ups, etc.)
- Learn their "language" – what makes them tick? Feed this into conversations

3. Build your personal marketing toolkit
- Polish your elevator pitch
- Brush up your social media profiles – find the right channels for you, it's better to be consistent than to be everywhere
- Organise your contacts – find a system that works and stick to it, remembering that small personal details about people help to build those relationships
- Research, research, research – before attending an event or a meeting, make sure you've done your homework. Check the guest list, look up any connections in common, and have some openers ready

↓ Elevator Pitch

Tell us about yourself and your business idea. You have 60 seconds – GO!

**Then... Practise it out loud
And... Leave them wanting more!**

- Who are you?
- What do you do?
- What's your USP?
- Key achievement to date?
- What are you looking for?

Networking in action

Give first

A good way to ease yourself into networking is to volunteer. You could devote some of your time to mentoring in an organisation or supporting young entrepreneurs. Perhaps you feel more comfortable sharing your learnings via social media or a blog, or hosting a giveaway to groups that interest you.

The art of cold emails

These can be daunting at first, but don't ever hesitate to reach out. Everybody wants to be helpful (if it's easy). Rather than suggesting a coffee or chat, have a relevant and actionable request. Keep it short and explain why you are reaching out in no more than five to ten lines.

Take to the stage!

Speaking on podcasts or at events are great ways to grow your network. Nurture relationships with hosts and organisers, or even host your own if you're feeling confident.

Ask questions

Don't hesitate to ask relevant questions during events; engaging with speakers is a great way to build relationships. Follow up with new connections after an event to cement those ties.

 I hate the word networking – it doesn't have to mean some sort of seminar where you wear a name tag. But going out to places where you bump into people, you meet people, who are also trying to work on the same dream, no matter what stage of their career they're at, is really beneficial."

Priya Ahluwalia

How to keep in touch

Networking isn't just about making new contacts, it's also about nurturing and sustaining long-term relationships.

It's important to not only approach people when you need something; sometimes it's good to simply check in. If you keep your communication genuine and open, you are more likely to build valuable connections.

For example, you could send them a relevant article: "Thought of you when I read this..." Or pass on your congratulations on a big win. Following and engaging with connections on social media, buying their products, attending events they host, giving word-of-mouth recommendations – these are all ways of bolstering new relationships.

Finally, remember to be kind and be patient. Networking is a people process after all.

↓ The art of the follow-up

DO
- Email after the event: "It was great to meet you..."
- Remind people where you met
- Say, "Looking forward to keeping in touch", rather than a specific "ask"
- Keep it simple, with low commitment expected of the other person

DON'T
- Leave it too late
- Be afraid to keep trying (use your judgement)
- Put all your eggs in one basket
- Be crushed by rejection

NICK JONES

The Creative Champion

3

Nick Jones
Founder of Soho House

You're a young London-based Brit about to live your dream of opening your first business in New York City – a members' club, your first outside the UK. It's still a building site, people are wearing hard hats. But you have a large "insider" dinner on site to generate excitement with the local crowd and start to build the all-important community on the ground. To your surprise, David Bowie suddenly walks up to you and says, "This New York club is a great idea, I'd like to buy it." Do you sell to him?

If you're Nick Jones, Founder of Soho House, you break it to him gently that the New York club is not for sale, but you'd happily give Mr Bowie the consolation of being an initial investor in Soho House New York. He gladly takes up your offer.

Nick is clearly a man who knows what creative people want – socially, professionally and creatively. When he founded Soho House, he envisioned something that hadn't existed before – a place for people across the creative sectors to meet, socialise, collaborate and, as has happened many times over, build businesses together. It's a first-of-its-kind space that members call home in 42 major cities around the world, starting in 1995 from a space above his restaurant in London's Soho.

The word "networking" is famously loathed within the creative sector, conjuring up images of people brazenly handing out business cards and ruthlessly using each other – a practice seen as a betrayal of creativity. However, "networking" is really just building relationships – absolutely essential for any entrepreneur, but particularly creative entrepreneurs for whom collaboration is oxygen, both for creative innovation and business support. Nick has turned the loathed term on its head, creating a space where true connection can happen authentically and with huge enthusiasm.

I spoke to Nick at Soho House Headquarters at 180 Strand in London.

↗ Nick at Shoreditch House, his first foray into East London. Based in a former tea-packing plant, it also provided one of London's first rooftop pools

↓ Nick Jones: Highlights

- Loved seeing his parents entertain their friends at home, with much joy and conviviality, and loved going grocery shopping with his mum
- Began career in hospitality aged 16 as a graduate trainee at Trusthouse Forte
- In 1992 opened Cafe Boheme in London's Soho – a big success with the Soho creative crowd
- In 1995 took over three adjoining Georgian townhouses to open Soho House on the three floors above Cafe Boheme

- 42 houses around the world, as well as restaurants, spas, cinemas, workspaces by Soho Works, an interiors brand called Soho Home and skincare ranges called Cowshed and Soho Skin
- 176,305 members worldwide, plus over 95,000 on the waiting list
- In 2017 awarded a Member of the Order of the British Empire (MBE) by Queen Elizabeth
- In 2021 Soho House's parent company went public with an IPO on the New York Stock Exchange

↗ Nick at the opening of
   the very first Soho House
   in Greek Street in 1995 in
   the yellow dining room

↑ The original Soho House
   in Greek Street, on the
   top three floors, above
   Nick's original restaurant
   Cafe Boheme

→ The door to Soho House
   Greek Street, unchanged
   for three decades.

Building Soho House

I've always loved a room full of people having a good time. Watching my mum and dad entertain at home, I saw how, with a nice atmosphere and nice people, you can have a really good time and not only meet people you know but also meet new people. You can have interesting conversations, and those conversations can lead to all sorts of other opportunities. To me, that's what I felt I always wanted to do, although I hadn't worked out specifically what shape that would take.

Around the time I was 16 and thinking of what job I might do, London was very limited as to where and when people could go out. There were either pubs or restaurants. Restaurants would open at lunch time and close in the afternoon and reopen in the evening and then be finished by 11 p.m. Pubs closed at 11 p.m. I thought, *There must be a different way of doing things*. It all felt like it was down to the people who operated the hospitality, and not about the customers. I thought, *People want to eat at 4 p.m. or they want to have a drink at 1 p.m. in the morning or they want to have breakfast* – and there were really no places open for that.

Reinventing hospitality and connection

I saw there was a great opportunity in Britain to do hospitality in a different way. After some false starts, I started Cafe Boheme in Soho. It was open from 8 a.m. until 3 a.m. in the morning. It was like a corner cafe in France: we got the food right and the service right, people could do whatever they wanted to do, and we had jazz in the afternoon. It was packed full of people. It was really the start of what Soho House was all about – a place where people came to meet. I could hear laughter and conversation, taking me back to my dream of a room full of people having a good time.

Soho House

Then I got a call from my landlord saying, "The space above Cafe Boheme has come free, why don't you rent it and open something upstairs?" It was three floors of different rooms across three Georgian houses. The entrepreneurial thing is to always go and have a look no matter what, even if you don't have the headspace or the money. When I saw the space I thought, *If I'm not going to do it, someone else is going to do it and that will annoy me.*

It was upstairs and just had one small door to get into it on Greek Street, so I figured it had to be a private members' club; it couldn't be a public restaurant as people wouldn't know about it. I didn't know about private members clubs, but it seemed obvious to me that this needed to be one.

It was in Soho – a neighbourhood full of film and TV people, where all the theatres are, bustling with actors – it was the creative area of London. So it was obvious that the membership should be for creative people. I didn't know lots of them, so I put together a committee of people in film and TV and other interesting, relevant people who then went out and found my first 500 members.

We opened Soho House as a home away from home. It opened at 8 a.m. and closed at 3 a.m., people could do all the things I wanted – lots of rooms full of interesting people having a good time. That was the basis of what Soho House was.

I always wanted our members to flourish professionally and socially. I wanted Soho House to be a place where they could do both. People didn't live in Soho; they came to Soho to work. They loved that they could just come in, they didn't have to eat or drink; they could come in on their own. It was a proper home away from home.

Betting the house on New York

The next really big move was New York. For a Brit, opening a business in New York is quite petrifying. It's a frightening city to go to, especially when you're a young Brit who was barely making ends meet back in the UK. But my members said, "Try and do it in New York."

There were like 90 reasons not to go to New York and probably 10 reasons to do it. You could have easily chosen not to do it – it was risky, you don't understand the market, you don't know the right people in New York, it's quite expensive, it's vicious, the unions and this and that. I thought I'd much rather give it a go and if it all blew up in my face – go back to London with my tail between my legs – because it would have taken London down as well, I would have lost the whole business – rather than not do it.

It was a huge risk, the UK business was still quite fragile, but that's how you expand, that's where you need to find an entrepreneurial spirit and the confidence to go off and do it. When I saw it was working in London, I saw there was an opportunity to do this in cities around the world, to create eventually a global membership, not just a one-city membership community. But I had to get past the first hurdle, which was New York. We opened in the Meatpacking District – which I now realise was quite radical at the time, as it was a

↑ The first Soho House in
  New York City, in a former
  warehouse in the
  Meatpacking District

→ Soho House Mexico City
  is the first location in
  Latin America and marks
  the brand as truly global

pretty sketchy neighbourhood then – I just liked that the rent was cheap!

TAKEAWAY | **When your business starts to work, when you have enough feedback and can see a successful template developing, always be thinking about whether there may be opportunities to replicate that template in new locations.**

So I did the whole thing over again – found the site, raised the money and luckily, it worked, it's now been open 20 years.

> **What Nick does best, that nobody else does, is bring people together with a great atmosphere and energy.**

Andrew Carnie, Soho House CEO

Going public and surviving the pandemic

We went public in 2021. We were expanding, and we wanted to carry on expanding and needed to raise money, so it seemed it was a sensible route. It was during the pandemic; that was an experience, trying to keep everything ticking over! Our whole business is about bringing people together, and all the houses

I'd built over so many years were all closed within a period of about 20 days. My determination was to take care of the people who work for us and our members.

When you're an entrepreneur, you have to prepare yourself for the unknown. Things can go terribly wrong. But we got through it, we went public, and that's been a great experience.

I've done everything led by our members

I've done everything because my members have led me there; my business has been built on what my members want. For example, in the very early days, within a few months of opening in London in January, it suddenly went very quiet in May. I thought, *Wow, that didn't last very long – I didn't expect the business to fail so quickly*. Then someone told me, "No, Nick, all of your members are at the Cannes Film Festival!" So, the next year we did a 10-day pop-up there which worked incredibly well – our members loved it and it became an annual tradition.

How to gather a global community of like-minded people

We've built our community slowly since 1995. Most of the members who joined then are still members today – including our original 500 members, who are still so important to us.

Community is what Soho House has always been about. In every new house, we set up a committee in that city who help us build the community on the ground through word of mouth, through people who want to be part of it, through people who really see the benefit and want it to be part of their life. In whatever new city we open, we have some incredibly interesting, relevant people there to add to our membership. So, when they turn up at 180 Strand in London (our headquarters), that just makes 180 Strand more interesting and more diverse.

TAKEAWAY **These are some key universal lessons on building a community, including having a soul at its core, engaging like-minded people to help you spread the word and ensuring you are – and stay – relevant to your community.**

← Soho Works is Soho House's network of serviced offices, featuring co-working spaces at eight locations around the world to encourage creative collaboration

It's a long period of time building up all of our members, you can't just go out and find everyone who wants to join the next membership club in one go; there needs to be a soul, a relevance, a history. Hopefully we've been able to do that at Soho House. When you go into a new city, we do a lot of pre-work. We operate a programme called "City without houses"

where, before we open a house, we try to understand the city. Those people usually lead us to a developer or a building, which leads us to opening a permanent house. Then you start with the founder members, then the founder members turn into annual members and suggest other members – and you're off.

Entrepreneurship is lonely at times. You might have your great team around you, but you're still having to make all the decisions. In my case, I had to make decisions on opening certain houses in certain cities, and it's all a risk. But you get into it, you understand the pattern, the flow – you can walk into a building and work out whether that would make a nice Soho House or not. You can spend time in a city and you can soon see if it's going to be a city where you can generate the membership you need to make a Soho House successful.

Making creatives feel at home in every city

You can be in Soho House Berlin, and you know you're in Soho House, but also you know you're in Berlin. That recognisability is important to me. I love design; I love creating the space. No two buildings are the same – they have different shapes, different sizes, different looks and feels, and every city we go into is different. And we always start with a fresh piece of paper.

 We don't say, "Oh, let's take that from London and put it in Berlin." Every time we open a new house, we try to make it better than the last one.

Supporting entrepreneurship

I love seeing people who don't necessarily have the opportunity to open a door meeting the people who can open that door for them, so they can flourish with the creativity they have. Besides this happening organically throughout the houses, we also make it happen through our mentoring schemes, which we have in every house.

We also have lots of events where people can meet each other, talk about their businesses, share knowledge and give recommendations. It's really important that people feel they're a member of something which is engaged in what they're doing, what their contemporaries are doing and what the next generation want as well.

↓ Passing on lessons learned

LEARNING FROM FAILURE
I think the ability to figure things out (and the confidence to know that you can) is really important. And just because something goes wrong doesn't mean you're a failure – things are always going to go wrong. It's a question of learning from it, pulling yourself up, dusting yourself down and doing it differently next time.

BIGGEST CHALLENGE YOU'VE OVERCOME?
There have been so many. Better than answering what the challenges have been, better to say how to deal with the challenges.

It's that, there's always a way around it – around the side or over the top – if you think it through, there's always a solution.

GO FOR IT
My best advice for aspiring creative entrepreneurs would be, "Go for it". Don't dwell on what I said about opening in New York, when there were maybe 90 reasons not to do it and 10 reasons to do it. There are always reasons not to do something, but there's always a reason to do something. Find that reason and hang on to it. Be determined and it will come up good.

Work-Life Balance

Work-life balance can sound like a tired oft-repeated phrase. But as any successful entrepreneur will tell you, it is crucial. Getting it right is vital for the happiness and health of both your personal life and your business.

It's all about balance

Thriving, not just surviving, is a hard goal to achieve as a creative entrepreneur. From those just setting up their businesses to those who've enjoyed great success, striking the elusive work-life balance is a daily challenge. Work out what "thriving" means to you – we are all different.

As a founder, it's healthy to be aware that this finely poised balance is in constant jeopardy. You won't always get it right; you'll miss important moments with friends or family and you'll choose your business over your sanity on many occasions. But a great first step is recognising the risks of letting the balance get too far out of sync.

The danger zone

In the danger zone, you are just surviving. You feel anxious, angry, overwhelmed, fearful, defensive, egotistical, etc. It's difficult to reason or empathise when you are in this state because all your energy is put towards "getting through".

Many of us experience negative feelings. Allowed to persist on a daily basis, these can lead to a "burnout loop", resulting in chronic stress and exhaustion.

It's a top priority for us all to nurture our mental health, and everyone will have their own ways of checking in with and looking after themselves – be that a good night's sleep, a yoga class, nourishing food, experiencing nature or hanging out with friends.

If you do find yourself slipping into the danger zone, try these techniques as a starter, but always seek professional help and support when needed:

- **Noticing** – As you go through your day, become aware of when you are in the danger zone. Notice what you are thinking, feeling and doing at that moment. Don't judge, just observe
- **Labelling** – Try to identify the negative emotions you're feeling. Once you've done that, label it and describe to yourself what's going on. Why are you feeling overwhelmed today? Research shows that labelling our emotions helps to reduce their power over us
- **Small steps** – By taking small, incremental steps, you can coax yourself out of being stuck in a situation. You might be saying to yourself, "I can't do this presentation", and tip towards the danger zone. A powerful way to break this feeling can be to say, "OK, but if I could do this, what would the first step be?" Or, "What's the smallest step I could take towards making this presentation happen?" The answer might be to ask for help, or simply to brainstorm with pen and paper

Survival guide for first-time entrepreneurs

- You know the drill: eat well, sleep well, exercise well, and you'll work well
- Lean on professionals and mentors to get outside advice – it's too easy to get stuck in your own head
- Talk to successful entrepreneurs who've been through it all before. They'll have tips and understanding, something which your family might find hard to offer if they've never started a business before
- Explore working with a business coach
- Remember, nobody went to their grave thinking, *I wish I'd worked harder in life*. But, they do end up thinking, *I wish I'd spent more time with my family and friends*. Don't let it slip through your fingers
- Take time out to reassess where you are and where you want to be. Even if it's just a weekend or a day, headspace gives you the opportunity to think more freely
- Don't forget to have fun and enjoy the start-up journey. Being an entrepreneur involves taking lots of risks, which can be stressful, but if you aren't enjoying yourself along the way, then what's the point? Enjoying the journey means you'll stay creative, which is ultimately what will grow your business and motivate your team.

LOOKING TOWARDS THE FUTURE

← "Filtered Rays" is Yinka
Ilori's first permanent
installation in Berlin,
Germany, featuring
a colourful canopy
of translucent discs

A word on AI

Generative AI is transforming the creative world at a pace and in ways that no one can fully comprehend – not even the people working at its forefront. While worthy of volumes (which would all be out of date in minutes), I want to outline some fundamental points.

First, Gen AI poses some profound challenges that need to be worked out urgently. All people need to control their likeness (e.g. actors) and their copyrighted content from unauthorised reproduction, copying and AI training. Resolutions to these issues are in progress and they can't come soon enough. And, as in all tech revolutions, there will inevitably be a painful shift – already underway – as a range of creative roles are taken over by Gen AI. This will be heart-breaking to watch.

But, as we've seen in every major revolution before (DVDs, music sampling), new tech capabilities create new opportunities. I visited NVIDIA in Silicon Valley to find out more from the horse's mouth. NVIDIA has been at the forefront of the AI revolution for a decade and is now the market leader by far. Best known for making the key chips (GPUs) powering AI, they are actually creating the wider AI development ecosystem. What I found there was an insight into the future that was breathtaking.

The essential takeaway is that Gen AI can be a transformative partner for creatives. First, it does away with the need to code. Think about how fundamentally game-changing that is. From just a simple text or voice request or showing it an image or video, Gen AI can produce text, images, audio, video and 3D objects. This lets creators bring work to life which they never could have imagined before, and exponentially more quickly.

It can be your brainstorming and prototyping partner. Instead of taking months for an architect to produce say 10 prototypes of a building or a screenwriter to write six potential endings to a screenplay, AI can produce hundreds of prototypes in a few minutes. Setting these creators free to make the judgement of which are best and providing many which they may never have thought of in the first place.

My biggest piece of advice from visiting NVIDIA? Gen AI is here now. To future-proof yourself and to discover amazing new possibilities, start using it. Experiment with the chatbots, e.g. OpenAI's ChatGPT4o has become more life-like and is considered a great workhorse. Anthropic's Claude3 is considered more intellectual and artsy. Check out the text-to-video-generation tools, e.g. Runway and OpenAI's Sora (still in testing). Sign up for AI newsletters (I like "One Useful Thing" from Wharton professor Ethan Mollick); follow OpenAI, Nvidia and others on Twitter and watch their new product demos; choose a few journalists to keep on your radar (I think Kevin Roose at *The New York Times* is good).

Finally, you may ask, might AI take over creativity from humans altogether? Human creativity largely comes from the imagination making unexpected connections. AI can connect the dots, but only the ones its probabilistic pre-set learning rules enable it to connect. It's only humans who can connect the unexpected dots to create something not generative, but truly original. I myself am going all in on the humans.

↓ NVIDIA's headquarters in Silicon Valley, their Endeavor Building; my photo taken on my visit there

> The big creative leaps forward will be generated by humans.

Strauss Zelnick,
Take-Two Interactive

The future for creative entrepreneurs

I hope you have enjoyed the journey this book has taken you on – hearing from these titans of the creative world in their own words and from a perspective you may likely not have heard before: how they've built their creative businesses.

I hope you've been able to take away inspiration and key advice from their unique wisdom. And most of all, that you've been able to see yourself in them, and therefore feel that you can do it too. In addition, and no less importantly, I hope that, as much as I have, you've enjoyed spending time with these extraordinary people, getting an insight into their world and getting to laugh, commiserate and learn with them.

As a complement, the Business Essentials give you helpful, actionable roadmaps, laying out the basics so that you can recognise and reinforce what you already know and see where you need to find out more and determine your priorities.

It's very exciting to see signs that attitudes may be changing with regards to creativity and entrepreneurship. Newer generations are finding it easier to embrace the idea that a sustainable business is not only necessary but empowering to pursue the full potential of their creative visions. This trend will be accelerated with the increased mainstream awareness that creativity can be a business, and a very successful one, which this book seeks to demonstrate. The stigma around commerce is hopefully on its way out.

It's also promising to see creative educational institutions starting to add modules on entrepreneurship and business into their courses on a regular basis.

More broadly, outside the creative sector, this book shows how commercially successful the sector is. Together we can further the understanding that creativity not only brings the world joy, information and entertainment, but that it is also a major contributor to the world's economy, and a rich ground within which to pursue a career. This in turn will allow parents to feel more secure about their children pursuing creative careers and also dissuade governments from cutting funding for creative education.

In the end, this book is for everyone; for those who are just beginning to start a creative business, or thinking about it, or wanting to refresh and reach a new stage, or those who are dreaming about their next move – even if that is not to start your own business, but to apply some of the learning about creativity and business set out in this book in your job and everyday life. I hope the learning and inspiration in this book help you along your way.

Finally, I wish you luck. Because, selfishly, I want to see the creativity that you put into the world.

Index

Acknowledgements

I would like to thank...

First and foremost, the remarkable entrepreneurs whose examples, advice and insights are the heart of this book. Thank you for being so generous with your time and for your shared passion for passing along your largely untold entrepreneurial stories to an audience who can be inspired and empowered by them.

Peter Davis Dailey for being the king of the bon mot, epic design and my heart. This book couldn't have happened without you.

Elizabeth Sheinkman, my über agent at PFD and dear friend, for seeing the potential of this book immediately and passionately guiding my vision to reality.

Praline for the groundbreaking design which beautifully conveys the stories we are telling in a way that innately understands our audience. David Tanguy and Maelle Christien, you are icons of design and collaboration.

Pete Jorgensen of Dorling Kindersley for the honour of suggesting I write this book and for leading your great DK team to make it happen, including Flo Ward who stuck with me even after she went to another publisher.

Amalia Agathou for keeping the home fires burning at Creative Entrepreneurs while also jumping in to help on the book. I couldn't have accomplished everything without your brilliant and loyal help.

Michael Craig-Martin for spontaneously and eloquently providing your very special eye-witness account of the rise of the Young British Artists (YBA) movement.

Debbie Masterson for getting Ted's approval of my dedication while he was fishing in Argentina.

Hans Ulrich Obrist for your world-leading understanding of tech and games and your generous introductions.

Lionel Barber for the drive-by international phone calls on key advice.

Jack Self for talking philosophy, Corbusier and creative entrepreneur curation from your holiday in the South of France while walking your baby.

My literary role models Joan Juliet Buck, Henry Mance of the *FT* and Dana Brown of *Airmail* – as I often slipped into my default boring technical written-word persona, thanks for helping me find my human voice again through your inspirational and extremely witty writing.

DK as a company for your commitment to visual media, which I've learned is rare within the "Big 5" publishing houses. You can't tell stories about creativity without images, so thank you DK for letting us showcase what's at the core of this book and what can, in turn, inspire people to embrace business.

Finally, all of my dear friends and family who have endured months on end of hearing about "that bloody book." You are so kind to have indulged, supported and listened to me and to have given me the best ideas. I love you.

Picture credits

Quotation credits

All quotations are credited to the interviewee featured in his or her respective chapter, except p6 and p9 from Apple, 'Think Different' commercial (1997); p27 (top) from interview with author Carolyn Dailey; p27 (bottom) from *The Wizard of Oz*, Victor Fleming (1939); p30 from thepolicycircle.org, 'The Creative Economy' (2023); p32 from interview with author Carolyn Dailey; p34 from interview with author Carolyn Dailey; p49 from *Rolling Stone*, 'The 250 Greatest Guitarists of All Time' (2023); p93 from *Little Women*, Great Gerwig (2019); p129 cited in *Forbes*, 'Mentoring: From The Ballpark To The Boardroom And Beyond' by John Baldoni (2020); p185 from interview with author Carolyn Dailey; p196 from interview with author Carolyn Dailey; p206 from Page Six, 'Soho House founder Nick Jones says cancer gave him fresh perspective' by Sara Nathan (2022); p215 from interview with author Carolyn Dailey.

Editors Millie Acers and Florence Ward
Designer James McKeag
Production Editor Siu Yin Chan
Production Controller Louise Minihane
Senior Acquisitions Editor Pete Jorgensen
Managing Art Editor Jo Connor
Managing Director Mark Searle
Project and Jacket Designers Praline

DK would like to thank Maëlle Christien and Beatrice Bianchet for their design expertise, Amalia Agathou for her editorial support and Caroline Curtis for proofreading and indexing.

First published in Great Britain in 2025 by
Dorling Kindersley Limited
DK, One Embassy Gardens, 8 Viaduct Gardens,
London, SW11 7BW

The authorised representative in the EEA is
Dorling Kindersley Verlag GmbH. Arnulfstr. 124,
80636 Munich, Germany

A CIP catalogue record for this book
is available from the British Library.
ISBN: 978-0-2416-5129-2

Printed and bound in China

www.dk.com

MIX
Paper | Supporting
responsible forestry
FSC
www.fsc.org   FSC™ C018179

This book was made with Forest Stewardship Council ™ certified paper – one small step in DK's commitment to a sustainable future.
Learn more at
www.dk.com/uk/information/sustainability